Key West & The Florida Keys
The Delaplaine
2020 Long Weekend Guide

Andrew Delaplaine

**NO BUSINESS HAS PAID A SINGLE PENNY OR GIVEN *ANYTHING*
TO BE INCLUDED IN THIS BOOK.**

Senior Editors - *Renee & Sophie Delaplaine*
Senior Writer - **James Cubby**
Restaurant Reviews by Sebastian Bond

Gramercy Park Press
New York London Paris

Copyright © by Gramercy Park Press - All rights reserved.

Please submit corrections, additions or comments to
<u>andrewdelaplaine@mac.com</u>

Key West & the Florida Keys: The Delaplaine Long Weekend Guide

TABLE OF CONTENTS

Chapter 1 - Why Key West & The Florida Keys? – 4
Transportation & Tips for Getting Around
Specific Information During Your Visit
Visitors' Centers

Chapter 2 – LODGING (includes Camping) – 10
Upper & Middle Keys - Lower Keys - Key West - Gay Guesthouses

Chapter 3 – RESTAURANTS – 33
Upper & Middle Keys - Lower Keys - Key West

Chapter 4 – NIGHTLIFE – 57
Upper & Middle Keys - Lower Keys - Key West

Chapter 5 – ATTRACTIONS – 63
Upper & Middle Keys - Lower Keys - Key West - Key West Charters – Tours

Chapter 6 – SHOPPING & SERVICES – 97
Upper & Middle Keys - Lower Keys - Key West -

GYMS – 106

INDEX - 107

Chapter 1
WHY KEY WEST & THE FLORIDA KEYS?

Most people's idea of a vacation involves sun, sand and sea. The Florida Keys have it all and more. If you are traveling to Key West, you must drive down at least once. After that one drive, you can fly down, but you have to experience this drive at least once in your life. It's not one of the most famous drives in the world for nothing.

The incomparable views of both the Atlantic Ocean and the Gulf of Mexico will accompany you throughout your drive. Sometimes, admiring these clear warm waters is not enough. Soon after you pass Key Largo in the Upper Keys, the urge to stop and jump into the water will strike you. No worries, there are plenty of areas along the way where you can pull over and do just that. At times, the water is so shallow you will be walking far out and the warm waters will barely reach knee level. Back in the days when I was an avid scuba diver, we'd stop two or three times along the drive to Key West, fill our tanks at one of the roadside scuba shops, and go diving that very minute.

Also along the way you will find attractions and activities for just about everyone. From shipwreck museums, to shopping, to haunted houses, to water sports.

Restaurants offer an abundance of seafood cooked up in a variety of ways. I try to make it a rule to avoid all meats when I go to the Keys. The seafood is so good, so fresh, and so well prepared (even in the simplest crab shack) that you really shouldn't be eating burgers and steaks.

Nightlife in the Keys pretty much means bars, bars and more bars. People here DO like to drink. And you'll still see "rummies" here and there. These are people who have given up on life and migrated to the Keys where the pace of life slows to a crawl, to a rum-induced haze.

Speaking of that pace, it's something you'll notice right away. Things do move at a much slower pace than most people are used to. Here, you will be forced to relax. Whether you want to or not. I remember once I was in a hurry to get to a party at the Pier house in Key West. I was flying down from my office in Miami. It was a hot, muggy summer night. I dashed out of the airport and hopped into a cab and told the driver to "Hurry! I need to get to the Pier House right away!" The bearded, aging, burned-out hippy driver looked at me in the rearview mirror and said, "Okay, then, I'll go the long way. There's no rush in Key West," he pontificated. And he poked along at 20 mph. I wanted to kill him, but I got the message. This was many years ago, before there were any hotel chain properties in Key West. Before things went "corporate." Back when it was real.

TRANSPORTARTION AND TIPS FOR GETTING AROUND

The Mile Marker Address System
Along US 1 (also called the Overseas Highway), you'll see these small green signs along the way that start when you leave Florida City at the top of the Keys, with Mile Marker 126. The last Mile Marker is MM 0, which is in Key West. Many businesses give their address as "MM 56," for instance, which mean Mile Marker 56.

Basic Tip
My rule for transport about the Keys is simple: if you're in Key West, you don't need a car. If you're exploring the Upper and Middle Keys, why then of course you can't do without one. So if you're flying into Key West, do not rent a car once you get there. You simply will not need one. Cabs are plentiful. And nothing is more than a 5-minute cab ride away.

Similarly, if I drive down to Key West, the minute I get there I park the car and leave it, using cabs throughout my stay. When it's busy, parking is a nightmare (just like it is on South Beach, where I live), so I'm never hassled trying to park if I use cabs.

However, if you are staying on some of the larger keys or in Key West, there will be a variety of scooter rental places available. These scooter rental places also offer a variety of golf cart rentals that can accommodate different size parties from 2 people up to 6.

Beware Speed Traps
A lot of municipalities along the Overseas Highway set up speed traps which are designed primarily to raise revenue from unsuspecting tourists. So you've been warned. They usually don't give a damn if you're 3 miles or 15 over the limit. They just want your money. One place where you really ought to slow down, however, is Big Pine Key where the **National Key Deer Refuge** is located. This is the habitat of a small population of "Key deer," a small (and very cute) animal that's in serious danger (150 were killed by cars last year).

SPECIFIC INFORMATION DURING YOUR VISIT

The best you can do here is just ask one of the friendly locals for events and local points of interest. Some of the larger keys have local publications that will offer information about events taking place during the time you are there.

http://hometownkeywest.com/events/

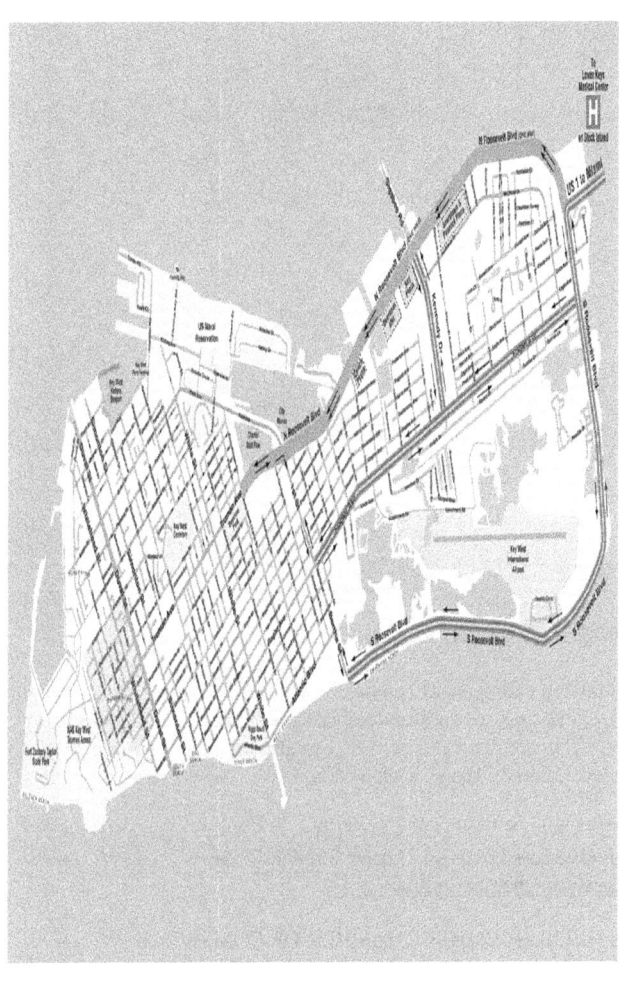

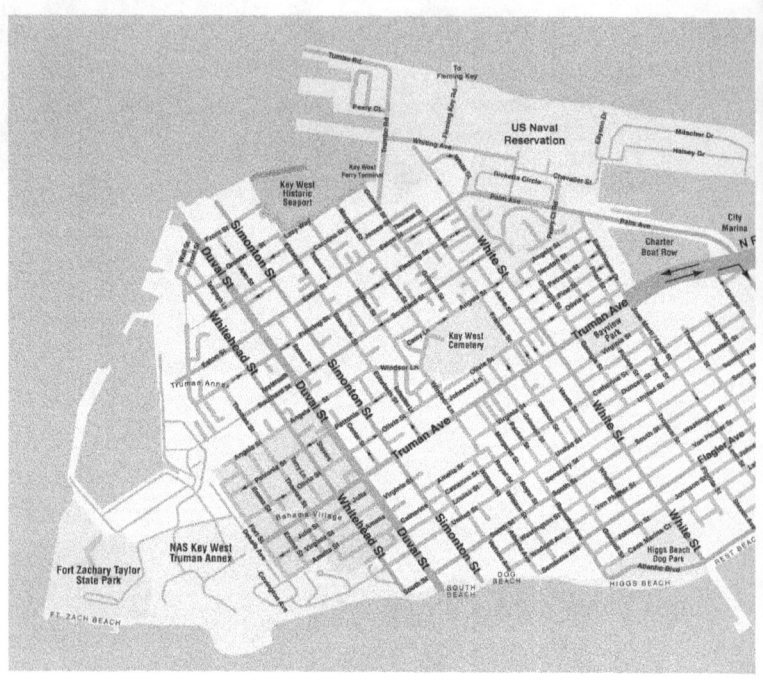

VISITOR'S CENTERS

The following chambers of commerce will provide specific information about local businesses and services along with discount coupons and promotions in the general area. You can also get maps and information on the local cultural scene, such as it is.

FLORIDA KEYS VISITOR CENTER
106240 Overseas Hwy, Key Largo, 305-712-6596
www.keylargochamber.org/about-us/

GREATER MARATHON CHAMBER OF COMMERCE
12222 Overseas Hwy, Marathon: 305-743-5417
www.floridakeysmarathon.com/

ISLAMORADA CHAMBER OF COMMERCE
87100 Overseas Hwy, Mile Marker 87, Bayside, 305-664-4503
www.islamoradachamber.com/

KEY LARGO CHAMBER OF COMMERCE

106000 Overseas Hwy, Key Largo: 305-451-1414
www.keylargochamber.org/about-us/

MONROE COUNTY TOURISM SITE
www.fla-keys.com/keylargo/

KEY WEST CHAMBER OF COMMERCE
510 Greene St., 1st Floor, Key West: 305-294-2587
www.keywestchamber.org/

LOWER KEYS CHAMBER OF COMMERCE
U.S. 1 at MM 31, Big Pine Key: 305-872-2411
www.lowerkeyschamber.com/

Chapter 2
LODGING
(includes Camping)

UPPER & MIDDLE KEYS

PRICEY

AMARA CAY RESORT
80001 Overseas Highway, Islamorada, 305-664-0073
www.amaracayresort.com
Elegant oceanfront resort (100 rooms and suites) known for comfort. You're right on the water, so it's got sandy beaches, that exquisite blue-green water you came to the Keys to splash around in. Perfect for diving, fishing, water sports. If you're coming down here to get away from it all, this is where you want to be. The restaurant here is Oltremare, and serves Italian cuisine that is good enough to keep you from having to get in the car to go somewhere else. Amenities include: free Wi-Fi, flat-screen TVs, coffeemakers and free continental breakfast. Hotel facilities include: outdoor heated pool, private beach,

poolside tiki bar, Bocce Ball courts, and on-site dive shop. A smoke-free property.

CASA MORADA
136 Madeira Rd., Islamorada: 305-664-0044
http://www.casamorada.com
Ultra chic (though with a laid-back attitude), this 16-room paradise is the Keys' answer to a boutique hotel. Tucked away on a serene street, some rooms offer open-air Jacuzzis that face the bay. Outdoor showers are great for cleansing the body and the soul. The lush garden was designed by Raymond Jungles. The bar on the bay is where you'll doubtless want to hang out with the other guests to take in the postcard perfect sunsets. If you use your cell phone, use it discreetly. No kids under 16, either, which is nice unless you're a parent with a kid under 16. You can borrow snorkeling gear to explore the shallow waters. This is one of those places in the Keys that make you wonder why the hell you don't go home, sell everything and move. Free breakfast daily and on Wednesdays, you can enjoy their free yoga.

CHEECA LODGE & SPA
81801 Overseas Hwy, MM 82, Islamorada: 305-664-4651
http://www.cheeca.com
Set on 27 acres of lushly landscaped beachfront, this laid-back resort offers a 9-hole Jack Nicklaus designed golf course. Enormous rooms open up to huge balconies with either ocean or island views; they contain spa tubs for two and glass rain showers. The resort offers babysitting, children's nature program, saltwater lagoon, full service spa and tennis courts.

FARO BLANCO RESORT & YACHT CLUB
1996 Overseas Hwy, Marathon, 305-743-1234
www.faroblancoresort.com
Newly reopened resort and full-service marina (that can handle boats of up to 120 feet) and yacht club offers 125 oversize stylishly decorated rooms and suites. Off the lobby is their **Market Gallery** that sells sandwiches, pizzas and other light fare 24/7 so you can always grab a bite at the last minute. Amenities include: free Wi-Fi, wide screen 42' TVs, and concierge service. On-site veranda bar. A variety of watersports available on the property. Good for families. Pet friendly.

HAWKS CAY RESORT
61 Hawk's Cay Blvd., Duck Key: 888-395-5539
http://www.hawkscay.com
In addition to many outdoor activities such as sailing, fishing, snorkeling, and water-skiing, this resort offers you the unique

experience of swimming with dolphins in their saltwater lagoon. Set on its own 60-acre island, here you will find a full service marina, spa, exercise room, clay and hard tennis courts. Ultra posh rooms with ocean views.

ISLANDER RESORT
82100 Overseas Hwy, Islamorada, 305-664-2031
www.islanderfloridakeys.com/
Relaxed Oceanside vacation spot offers a relaxed resort atmosphere with twenty-five contemporary cottages. Amenities include: free Wi-Fi, full gourmet kitchens, and flat-screen TVs. Resort facilities include: two outdoor pools, private beach, fitness center, and on-site bar & grill. Conveniently located near attractions like the History of Diving Museum.

JULES' UNDERSEA LODGE
51 Shoreland Dr., Key Largo: 305-451-2353
http://www.jul.com
Truly a unique experience, this research lab turned lodge offers guests an opportunity to stay – underwater. To get inside, guests swim 21 feet under the structure and pop up into the unit. Room service, daily newspapers, and even a late-night pizza will be delivered in waterproof containers. You think I'm kidding, right? Look at their web site.

KONA KAI RESORT & GALLERY
97802 Overseas Hwy., Key Largo: 305-852-7200
http://www.konakairesort.com

An adults-only retreat, this property offers stunning sunset views over Everglades National Park. Rooms are modern with lots of style. Take advantage of their private beach or ask the concierge to organize an excursion into the 'Glades. Boat dockage available.

THE MOORINGS VILLAGE
123 Beach Rd., Islamorada: 305-664-4708
http://www.themooringsvillage.com
Only 18 small cottages are on this old coconut plantation, but if you stay in one, you'll get a pure Keys experience. A Frenchman who saw the 18-acre spot as he windsurfed by it in 1988 bought the place. It's just a few cottages in the hammocks surrounded by some 700 soaring palm trees and sand. On the private beach, you can get stand-up paddleboards and kayaks. Bikes available.

MORADA BAY BEACH CAFÉ
81600 Overseas Hwy, Islamorada, 305 664-3225
www.moradabay.com/the-beach-cafe
Across the road from the Moorings is this place, a good spot for tropical cocktails and conch fritters in a laid-back atmosphere of painted chairs and tiki torches stuck in the sand. Or get something like stone crabs to go and a six-pack of cold beer and each on the porch of your cottage. 1,100-foot private beach and tennis courts.

TRANQUILITY BAY BEACH HOUSE RESORT
2600 Overseas Hwy., Marathon: 305-289-0888
http://www.tranquilitybay.com
Situated on the Gulf of Mexico, this newer resort offers all the amenities including a private spa, lagoon pools and a great lawn. There is also an adventure kids' club. This is a non-smoking resort.

MODERATE

BANANA BAY RESORT & MARINA
4590 Overseas Hwy. at MM 49.5, Marathon: 305-743-3500
http://www.bananabay.com
Not much from the outside but once you step inside this property, you will realize how lush and relaxing it is. Activities include horseshoe pits, a bocce court, barbecue grills, and a giant lawn chessboard. Many of the rooms have private balconies. This family friendly resort offers one of the largest fresh water pools in the Keys.

COCONUT PALM INN
198 Harborview Dr. at MM 92, Tavernier: 305-852-3017
http://www.coconutpalminn.com
Former fish camp, this inn is located on a private white sand beach. All rooms have delightful bay views. Heated fresh water pool and free WiFi, even on the beach.

LITTLE CONCH KEY PRIVATE ISLAND ESCAPE
62250 Overseas Hwy. at MM 62.3, Marathon: 305-289-1377
http://www.conchkeycottagesfloridakeys.com/
Get ready to play castaway on this private island. All cottages, this is truly the place to get away from it all when you stay in one of their two-bedroom stilt cottages. Free Continental breakfast and free use of kayaks. Heated pool and free WiFi.

POSTCARD INN BEACH RESORT & MARINA
84001 Overseas Hwy. at MM 84, Islamorada: 305-664-2321
http://www.holidayisle.com
Attracting a Spring Break kind of crowd, both locally and from afar this is home to the famous **Tiki Bar**. If you like noisy partying and merrymaking, you will feel right at home. Don't expect much from the rooms, but then again, is that really why you're here? When it's not Spring Break, of course, the place is a tad more laid back (like the rest of the Keys), so it's just fine. Also is home to **Shula Burger**, which is the first in a new restaurant chain launched by the legendary Miami Dolphins coach. (Other locations are opening soon in Delray, Lauderdale, Miami and Tampa.) I like to hang out at **Jaw's Raw Bar** for the oysters and raw clams.

LIME TREE BAY RESORT MOTEL
U.S. 1 at MM 68.5, Long Key: 305-664-4740
http://www.limetreebayresort.com
Located in the tiny town of Layton, this is a no-frills little motel with great views. Large private deck overlooking the Gulf, but better yet, no bartenders in Hawaiian shirts!

PINES AND PALMS
80401 Old Hwy. at MM 80.4, Islamorada: 800-624-0964
http://www.pinesandpalms.com
Cozy cottages with Atlantic views and a private beachfront with hammocks make this a true tropical paradise. All rooms and cottages have full kitchens and balconies and even though there is no on-site restaurant, you can always grill out by the beach. This place is ideal for extended stays.

INEXPENSIVE

JOHN PENNEKAMP CORAL REEF STATE PARK
102601 Overseas Hwy at MM 102.5, Key Largo: 305-451-6300
http://www.pennekamppark.com
If camping is your thing, this is the place to go. Tent sites are small but equipped with restrooms, hot water and showers. Here you will find two small beaches and a lagoon. Bring insect repellent. (See the extensive listings in the **Attractions chapter** for all the super things to do here at Pennekamp.)

LONG KEY STATE PARK
U.S. 1 at MM 67.5, Layton: 305-664-4815
http://www.abfla.com/parks/longkey/longkey.html

Being more secluded that John Pennekamp State Park makes this campsite more popular. All sites are located ocean side and have nearby restroom facilities. If you plan on visiting in winter, make reservations well in advance.

RAGGED EDGE RESORT
243 Treasure Harbor Rd. at MM 86.5, Islamorada: 305-852-5389
http://www.ragged-edge.com
Small oceanfront property with a Tahitian theme, this place is kept immaculately clean and is very comfortable. There is no restaurant, bar, or staff to speak of really but the owner is more than willing to point you in the right direction of nearby venues.

LODGING LOWER KEYS

INEXPENSIVE

PARMER'S RESORT
565 Barry Ave, Summerland Key: 305-872-2157
http://www.parmersresort.com
Modest but comfortable cottages, this place is charming and has a very helpful staff. Some units are waterfront and most have kitchenettes. Only a half hour drive to Key West. Extra charge for maid service.

LODGING KEY WEST

AMBROSIA KEY WEST
622 Fleming St., Key West: 305-296-9838
http://www.ambrosiakeywest.com
Private compound set on 2 lush acres just one block from Duval Street. Property has three lagoon-style pools and rooms vary from suites to townhouses and cottages. All rooms have private entrances, most with French doors that give you the feeling that the landscaping is part of your room. Property offers variety of intimate outdoor spaces, including private verandas; patios; and gardens with sculptures and fountains. Great service.

ANGELINA GUEST HOUSE
302 Angela St., Key West: 888-303-4480
http://www.angelinaguesthouse.com
Former bordello and gambling hall, it is now a youth hostel and one of the cheapest in town. Set in an urban neighborhood, it is definitely safe and full of character. Modestly appointed, only four of their rooms have private baths. Gorgeous pool with poolside hammocks. Great place to stay if traveling on the cheap.

BANYAN RESORT
323 Whitehead St., Key West: 305-296-7786
http://www.thebanyanresort.com
Cute, historic building located within walking distance of everything. Very limited parking available. Management tends to be somewhat unaccommodating at times. Mini kitchens and dishes in rooms. Free WiFi.

BEACHSIDE RESORT & CONFERENCE CENTER
Key West Marriott Beachside Hotel
3841 N. Roosevelt Blvd., Key West: 305-296-8100
www.beachsidekeywest.com
Acclaimed chef **Norman Van Aken** heads two restaurants on the property. Two and three bedroom suites as well as king rooms available, all waterfront with private balconies. Private sundecks available on the third floor.

BLUE MARLIN MOTEL
1320 Simonton Street, Key West: 305-294-2585
http://bluemarlinmotel.com

Blue Marlin Motel, located in the South Beach area (a block from the water), features 57 large guestrooms with cable TV, refrigerator, microwave and coffee maker. Just one block off Duval Street - walking distance to all attractions, restaurants, bars and beaches. A large heated pool is the centerpiece of the property. Families are welcome here. Free parking.

CABANA INN
413 Applerouth Lane, Key West: 866-413-2230
www.thecabanainn-keywest.com
It's one big happy family here. Attentive service and pampering within lush landscaping with rainforest shower and open-air patio. Fitness center. At Cabana Inn they offer 6 separate buildings all enclosed in one very large compound. The numerous guest rooms have various shape and styles. We have rooms that may accommodate from 1 to 6 persons all at different sizes and rates. Full breakfast included.

CASA MARINA RESORT & BEACH CLUB
1500 Reynolds St., Key West: 305-296-3535
http://www.casamarinaresort.com
Complete renovation offers historic architecture with modern Key West. Large private beach, sweeping lawns and a grand veranda. Two outdoor pools and a full service spa. Free movies with popcorn and snacks shown nightly by the pool.

CHELSEA HOUSE
709 Truman Ave., Key West: 305-296-2211
www.historickeywestinns.com/the-inns/chelsea-house
This historic Key West hotel, located in Old Town area just two blocks from Duval Street, includes two grand Victorian mansions set on an acre of tropical gardens. All guestrooms include private bath with

shower, cable TV, telephone, and air conditioning. Amenities include: heated pool, lounging areas, free continental breakfast, free parking, and free wireless internet access in the courtyard.

CROWNE PLAZA LA CONCHA
430 Duval St., Key West: 305-296-2991
www.laconchakeywest.com
A National Historic Landmark located in the heart of the Historical District. Since its opening in 1926, this legendary hotel has welcomed an impressive list of guests including Ernest Hemingway and Tennessee Williams. All beautifully-decorated and richly-appointed guestrooms & suites include: 42" Flat Screen TVs, CD Player & Clock Radio, Coffee/Tea Maker, Free newspaper and toiletries, and free high-speed wireless access. Amenities include: swimming pool, fitness center and gift shop.

CURRY MANSION INN
511 Caroline St., Key West: 305-294-5349
http://www.currymansion.com
Former home of the island's first millionaire, now listed in the National Register of Historic Places. Rooms are minimally decorated in a warm, friendly way. European style breakfast buffet is included along with evening cocktail parties.

CYPRESS HOUSE
601 Caroline St., Key West: 305-294-6969
www.historickeywestinns.com/the-inns/cypress-house
This historic Key West inn, located in the Old Town area, is set inside a lush, tropically landscaped, gated property. 22 guestrooms are located in buildings that are over 120 years old but of course have been updated with new furnishings and modern amenities including private bath, flat-screen TV, and wireless internet service. Free daily continental

breakfast, poolside refreshments, and evening cocktail with light appetizers. Guests enjoy lounging by the 40-foot, heated lap pool. Adults only.

DOUBLETREE BY HILTON GRAND KEY RESORT
3990 S. Roosevelt Blvd., Key West: 305-293-1818
www.doubletreekeywest.com
This luxury hotel welcomes guests with a freshly baked chocolate chip cookie. Conveniently located just a mile from the beach, the golf course, and the airport. Lounge by the beautiful pool with waterfall, whirlpool, and large sunbathing decks. On site Palm Haven Restaurant and poolside Tiki Bar. Free WiFi high-speed internet access.

DUVAL INN
511 Angela St., Key West: 305-295-9531
www.duvalinn.com
This turn-of-the-century historic guesthouse offers all the comforts and details of a modern hotel. Amenities include secluded pool, cable TV, phone, minibar, Free island breakfast and happy hour. Free Wi-Fi internet access.

EDEN HOUSE
1015 Fleming St., Key West: 305-296-6868
http://www.edenhouse.com
With beautifully landscaped grounds complete with waterfalls and porch swings, this place has some rooms that are semi-private (shared bathrooms). Free happy hour from 4–5. Amenities include pool, Jacuzzi, sundeck and grill area. 39 rooms scattered among vintage buildings around a shared courtyard. Nightly free cocktail hour.

FAIRFIELD INN & SUITES
2400 N. Roosevelt Blvd., Key West: 305-296-5700
www.fairfieldinnkeywest.com
A Marriott owned hotel that offers 106 comfortable guest rooms & suites. Amenities include: on-site scooter rentals, in-room refrigerators and microwaves, flat screen TVs, free high-speed internet access, customized showers, free parking and deluxe continental breakfast. Lounge by the beautiful 72,000-gallon free-form pool with Tiki Bar.

THE GARDENS HOTEL
526 Angela St., Key West: 800-526-2664
http://www.gardenshotel.com
Once a private residence, this hotel is listed on the National Register of Historic Places. Luxury appointed rooms amidst luscious landscaping. Rooms have hardwood floors, brass iron beds and marble bathrooms. Free form pool located in center courtyard and Jacuzzi is hidden behind stunning foliage.

THE GATES HOTEL
3824 N Roosevelt Blvd, Key West, 305-320-0930
www.gateshotelkeywest.com
Though it calls itself a boutique hotel, it's got over 100 rooms, but these are all modern accommodations. It's located where US 1 enters Key West, so it's as far from Old Town as you can get. Amenities include: free Wi-Fi, flat-screen TVs, designer toiletries and free bottled water. Hotel features include: pool, bar, and lounge. Great relaxed Key West atmosphere with live music.

THE GRAND GUESTHOUSE
1116 Grinnell St., Key West: 305-294-0590
https://thegrandguesthouse.com/

Undoubtedly the best bargain in town, this place is located just five blocks from Duval Street. A classic bed and breakfast located in the Old Town neighborhood within walking distance to shops, restaurants, museums, beaches and nightlife. All rooms have private bathrooms and entrances, queen size beds, A/C & ceiling fans, cable TVs, iPod, iPhone, and CD players, and refrigerator. All rooms are non-smoking. Free Continental breakfast. Free parking and high speed wireless internet access.

HYATT CENTRIC KEY WEST RESORT & MARINA
601 Front St., Key West: 305-809-1234
https://keywest.centric.hyatt.com
Located near Duval Street, this hotel is close to some very lively bars. Great spa offering a new green certified skin-care line. With a private beach, it has watersports equipment rental on premises.

ISLAND CITY HOUSE HOTEL
411 William St., Key West: 305-294-5702
http://www.islandcityhouse.com
Oldest running B&B in Key West, it consists of three buildings that share a lushly landscaped pool and patio. Continental breakfast is included.

KEY WEST MARRIOTT BEACHSIDE HOTEL
3841 N. Roosevelt Blvd., Key West: 305-296-8100
www.beachsidekeywest.com
This Marriott resort hotel, set on seven lush acres with a tanning beach and waterfront pool, is one of the highest rated Key West hotels in the Keys. The hotel features 129 one, two and three bedroom suites with with gourmet kitchens, spa tubs, living room and balcony; plus 93 king standard rooms all with free high speed internet access. On site dining options include Tavern N' Town and the poolside Blue Bar. Free airport and downtown hotel shuttle. Acclaimed chef **Norman Van Aken** heads two restaurants on the property.

KNOWLES HOUSE B&B
1004 Eaton St., Key West: 305-296-8132
www.knowleshouse.com
An award-winning Key West inn, set in the historic Old Town district, offers an authentic Key West guesthouse experience in an elegant, yet homey atmosphere. Conveniently located just five blocks from the action on Duval Street but far enough away so you can enjoy the serenity of an island retreat. Amenities include: Free Continental breakfast, pool, Jacuzzi, rooftop sundeck and spacious back porch. Full concierge services available.

LA PENSIONE
809 Truman Ave., Key West: 800-893-1193
http://www.lapensione.com
Classic B&B in an 1891 home has lots of charm. Rooms do not have TVs but it is only steps away from Duval Street. Breakfast is included, free WiFi. Bike rental on premises.

LA TE DA
1125 Duval St., Key West: 305-296-6706
www.lateda.com
This is a wonderful place to stay, certainly one of my all-time favorites in Key West. Comfortable lodgings in an old white clapboard house that just screams "Old Key West." Definitely check out their web site. Even if you don't stay here, you must drop by for dinner or to hang out in their elegant bar. Sit outside under the trees if the weather's good. The place turns magical at night. (See listing in restaurant section.)

LIGHTHOUSE COURT
902 Whitehead St., Key West: 305-294-9588
www.historickeywestinns.com
A historic guest inn, just one block off Duval Street, is conveniently located next door to the Key West Lighthouse Museum and across the street from the Ernest Hemingway Home and Museum. The inn is comprised of ten "conch" buildings dating back from 1890 to the 1920s housing forty guestrooms. The grounds are filled with tropical landscaping, brick pathways and decked courtyards offering many areas for lounging and sunning. Guests can lounge by the large pool in the main courtyard while sipping on cocktails from the Mojito Bar & Café. Free wireless internet service is available around the courtyard. Free breakfast is served daily in the courtyard.

MARGARITAVILLE RESORT & MARINA
245 Front St., Key West: 305-294-4000
www.margaritavillekeywestresort.com
This resort is located on the waterfront, just one block from the infamous Duval Street and next to Mallory Square. As the only full-service resort to receive the AAA Four-Diamond rating every year since 1999, you're guaranteed excellent service. The resort features deluxe guestrooms and suites, multiple dining options, heated pool and a 37-slip marina. Amenities include: 24-hour room service, free wireless high-speed internet access, 24-hour fitness room, massage studio, and concierge services.

THE MARKER WATERFRONT RESORT
200 William St, Key West, 305-501-5193
www.themarkerkeywest.com
Newly built (in 2014) waterfront hotel features 96 state-of-the-art rooms located on two beautifully landscaped acres in that part of Key West that used to be dominated by dive bars and shrimp boats. The conch-style design elements used in this property help make it fit right in. This is the first new hotel built in Old Town in a couple of decades. Perfectly located just a couple of blocks off Duval Street. If you want to be away from it all, this is not the place for you. Like all the lodgings in this part of town, it's great for stumbling home drunk from the bars

late at night. Amenities include: free Wi-Fi, flat-screen TVs, minibars, and private balconies. Hotel facilities include: 3 outdoor pools, fitness center, on-site restaurant and bar, poolside beverage service, and bicycle rental. Smoke-free hotel.

MARQUESA HOTEL
600 Fleming St., Key West: 305-292-1919
http://www.marquesa.com
Small historic hotel with large resort amenities. Sumptuously restored, the décor in these Victorian homes have achieved the perfect balance of posh antiques and contemporary furniture. The bathrooms are typically large and the property also offers two pools with waterfalls. Their Marquesa restaurant is one of the best on the island

THE MERMAID & THE ALLIGATOR B&B
729 Truman Ave., Key West: 305-294-1894
www.kwmermaid.com
This beautiful 1904 Victorian home, located in the heart of Old Town Key West, offers the warm hospitality of a traditional bed & breakfast. Relax in a beautiful garden setting or stroll along Duval Street- just three blocks away. All guest rooms feature exquisite accommodations with high-speed wireless Internet access. Free breakfast and evening glass of wine. Heated plunge pool with whirlpool jets. Concierge service available.

OCEAN KEY RESORT AND SPA
One Duval St., Key West: 800-328-9815
http://www.oceankey.com

Located at the foot of Mallory Square, the epicenter of the sunset ritual. Their Sunset Pier allows guests to enjoy cocktails and live music. Huge, luxuriously appointed rooms. Indonesian inspired spa and their restaurant, Hot Tin Roof, is one of the best in Key West.

OLD TOWN MANOR & ROSE LANE VILLAS
511 Eaton St., Key West: 305-292-2170
www.oldtownmanor.com
Here you have two properties, Old Town Manor & Rose Lane Villas, offering a bed & breakfast experience just steps from the busy Duval Street. Amenities include free wireless internet access and a healthy all-natural breakfast. Pet friendly and a state certified Green lodging.

PIER HOUSE RESORT & CARIBBEAN SPA
1 Duval St., Key West: 305-296-4600
http://www.pierhouse.com
At the foot of Duval Street, this legendary property is walking distance to everything. Has a short strip of private beach. Rooms vary from simple business-style rooms to romantic, intimate lodgings with whirlpool tubs. Every room has a private balcony or patio but not all have water views. Once upon a time, this was THE place to stay in Key West (unless you opted for the guesthouse style lodging). The place was built by the famously eccentric David Wolkowski, who opened it in 1968. I can't tell you how many famous people I used to see in the Chart Room Bar and restaurants of this place over the years (but mainly back in the '70s and '80s), from Tennessee Williams in his Panama hat sauntering down Duval Street with his latest boy-toy to lesser luminaries. And though the Pier House has gone very "corporate," it's still one of my favorite places on the island. (I looked on the web site, and there isn't even a mention of David Wolkowski's name. Whoever the new owners are, this shows extremely poor taste!)

THE REACH RESORT
1435 Simonton St., Key West: 305-296-5000
http://www.reachresort.com

Just a 5-minute walk from Duval Street, the rooms are large and have a modern tropical décor. Rooms have sliding glass doors that open up to balconies, some with ocean views. Large array of watersports available on premises.

SAINT HOTEL KEY WEST
417 Eaton St, Key West, 305-294-3200
www.thesainthotelkeywest.com
Located in Key West Historic District, this hotel offers 36 comfortable rooms. Amenities include: free Wi-Fi, free continental breakfast, and TVs with cable channels. Hotel features include: outdoor pool, bar/lounge, and garden. Located near attractions like Mallory Square and Ernest Hemingway Home and Museum.

SANTA MARIA SUITES
1401 Simonton St., Key West: 305-296-5678
www.santamariasuites.com
A sophisticated, contemporary resort located less than a block from the ocean and Duval St. The Suites offers refined luxury accommodations with spacious suites with private balconies and terraces. Two-bedroom suites are also offered. Full concierge services available. Two garden-enclosed heated pools. Ambrosia Restaurant (on site) serves sushi and Japanese cuisine. Free parking.

SEASCAPE
420 Olivia St., Key West: 800-765-6438
http://www.seascapetropicalinn.com
Tucked away behind the Hemingway House, this retreat has a colorful history being built in the Bahamas and transported by ship where it was re-built in Key West. Most rooms have French doors that open up onto

a heated pool and Jacuzzi. Within walking distance to the water and nightlife.

SEASHELL MOTEL & KEY WEST INTERNATIONAL HOSTEL
718 South St., Key West: 305-296-5719
http://www.keywesthostel.com
A five-minute walk to the beach and old town, this hostel offers all male, all female or co-ed facilities. Busy with traveling backpackers, this is a great place to meet people. Great deals for breakfast, lunch and dinner. Free WiFi.

SILVER PALMS INN
830 Truman Ave., Key West: 305-294-8700
www.silverpalmsinn.com
This historic Old Town boutique hotel, just three blocks from Duval Street, offers island charm and comfortable accommodations. Amenities include: Free daily continental breakfast, free Wi-Fi and Wired internet, free parking, and Fitness Room. The Inn features brand new beautifully appointed guest rooms with modern island décor. Heated pool.

SIMONTON COURT HISTORIC INN & COTTAGES
320 Simonton St., Key West: 800-944-2687
http://www.simontoncourt.com
Once a cigar factory, this charming inn features luxurious gardens and four pools. Lodgings include the bed and breakfast, cottages, guesthouse, mansion and inn all housed on one large property. (Some of these properties housed workers in the old factory.) Located just around the corner from Duval Street in the heart of Old Town. Families take note, as this is an adults only resort with excellent service.

SOUTHERNMOST BEACH RESORT
1319 Duval St., Key West: 305-296-6577
www.southernmostresorts.com
Southernmost, located in the heart of historic old town and across the street from the beach, is just steps from the busy nightlife of Key West. Giant pool, on site spa, resort activities and fitness classes, and four restaurants (Southernmost Beach Café, Shores Bar
Southernmost on the Beach, Sand Bar Southernmost on the Beach, and The Pineapple Bar).

SOUTHERNMOST HOUSE
1400 Duval St., Key West: 305-296-3141
www.southernmosthouse.com
This architectural icon has welcomed Presidents and Kings and continues to welcome guests in the landmark hotel. This premier bed and breakfast offers 18 unique guestrooms. Amenities include: Free Island Style Continental breakfast, ocean side zero degree entry heated pool, pool bar, concierge services, and Free wireless internet.

SOUTHERNMOST POINT GUEST HOUSE
1327 Duval St., Key West: 305-294-0715
http://www.southernmostpoint.com
Pet and kid friendly, this quaint little inn also offers amenities for adults. Every room comes with fresh flowers, wine and sherry. You can also enjoy free wine in the 14-seat hot tub. Chairs and towels for the beach are provided. Kids will enjoy the backyard swings and pet rabbits.

SPEAKEASY INN
1117 Duval St., Key West: 305-296-2680
www.speakeasyinn.com
This recently renovated landmark inn, an elegant and romantic retreat, was the home of Raul Vaquez, a cigar selector at the Gato cigar factory and known fo his rum-running between Key West and Cuba. The inn offers one, two, and three bedroom accommodations that feature handcrafted queen beds, color TV, A/C, refrigerators, microwaves, and private baths. The popular Rum Bar is located in the lobby.

TRAVELERS PALM
815 Catherine St., Key West: 305-304-1751
www.travelerspalm.com
The Palm feature three all-new conch-style cottages nestled in lush tropical gardens that surround the solar-heated pool. Located just three blocks from the excitement of Duval Street. Cottages have private Jacuzzis and off-street parking. Amenities include: air conditioning, free wi-fi, and daily maid service. The Palm is also a state-of-the-art, eco-friendly certified Green Lodging.

TRUMAN HOTEL
611 Truman Ave., Key West: 305-296-6700
http://www.trumanhotel.com
Located in a quiet section just a block off the south end of Duval Street, this is one of the few really modern places in town. Very nicely decorated. The courtyard and pool area make a comfy place to read, sun, or visit with friends. Continental breakfast is served ever morning.

VILLAS KEY WEST
512 Angela St., Key West: 305-296-7893
www.villaskeywest.com
Villas Key West offer a charming selection of suites, cottages and rental homes. Villas range from a single room with a private bath to a two story, two bedroom/two bath villa with a private deck. All villas feature a custom kitchen. This quiet respite is just 200 feet from the bustling excitement of Duval Street.

WESTWINDS INN
914 Eaton St., Key West: 844-308-0080
http://www.westwindskeywest.com

Just four blocks from Duval Street, this property encompasses five separate buildings. Rooms are comfortable with private bathrooms, all non-smoking. Extremely private and secluded.

GAY GUESTHOUSES

ALEXANDER'S GUESTHOUSE
1118 Fleming St., Key West: 305-294-9919
http://www.alexanderskeywest.com
Each room is uniquely decorated in a warm, casual style. Some rooms have private verandas or decks.

EQUATOR RESORT
822 Fleming St., Key West: 305-294-7775
http://www.equatorresort.com
Comfortable, elegant and welcoming; guestrooms are clean and have spacious bathrooms. Clothing optional pool and daily happy hour. Breakfast is included.

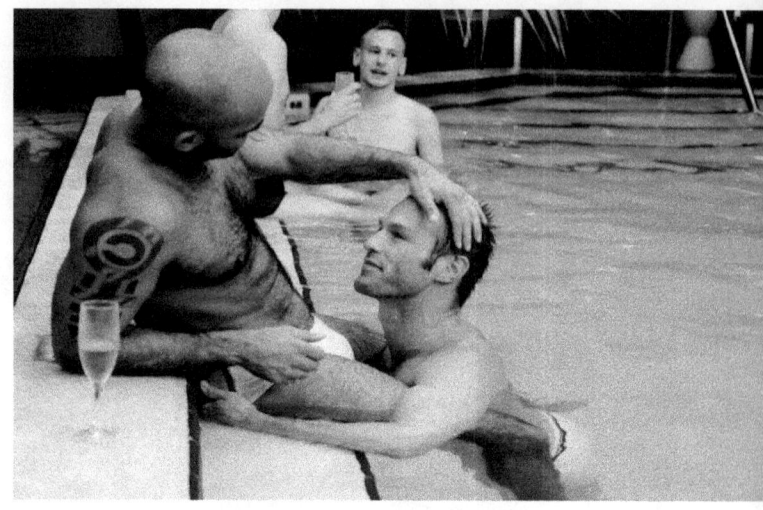

ISLAND HOUSE FOR MEN
1129 Fleming St., Key West: 305-294-6284
http://www.islandhousekeywest.com
Private, enclosed clothing optional compound. The amenities include large heated pool, indoor and outdoor Jacuzzis, gym, steam room, sauna, poolside cafe/bar, restaurant and erotic video room. Friendly staff.

NEW ORLEANS HOUSE
724 Duval St., Key West: 305-293-9800
http://www.neworleanshousekw.com
In the heart of old town Key West, this facility offers an all male clothing optional guest house with a variety of rooms, some opening out to the grand balcony overlooking Duval St., or the private sun deck, pool, hot tub and garden bar area.

Chapter 3
RESTAURANTS
UPPER & MIDDLE KEYS

ALABAMA JACKS
58000 Card Sound Rd., Key Largo: 305-248-8741
No web site
CUISINE: Seafood
DRINKS: Full bar
SERVING: Daily lunch and dinner
PRICE RANGE: $
One of the best places in all the Keys for conch fritters, certainly in the Upper Keys. Don't let the bikers at the other tables scare you. They're pretty much harmless unless you speak out of turn.

BARRACUDA GRILL
4290 Overseas Hwy. at MM 49.5, Marathon: 305-743-3314
www.barracuda-grill.com/
CUISINE: American/ Seafood
DRINKS: Beer/ Wine
SERVING: Dinner
PRICE RANGE: $$$-$$$
Small and casual, this spot serves really good seafood, steaks and chops. They offer a well-priced wine list of California wines. No reservations required.

BUTTERFLY CAFÉ
Tranquility Bay Beach House Resort
2600 Overseas Hwy., Marathon: 305-289-7177
http://www.tranquilitybay.com
CUISINE: Seafood
DRINKS: Beer/ Wine
SERVING: Breakfast/ Lunch/ Dinner
PRICE RANGE: $$-$$$
Inside the Tranquility Bay Resort, this place offers incredible water views and an even better menu. The Sunday brunch is particularly good.

CALYPSO'S SEAFOOD GRILL
1 Seagate Blvd. at MM 99.5, Key Largo: 305-451-0600
http://calypsoskeylargo.com/index.html
CUISINE: Seafood
DRINKS: Beer/ Wine
SERVING: Lunch/Dinner
PRICE RANGE: $
Typical Keys eatery on the water with loud music and good food. The she-crab soup is a must. Other specialties are cracked conch and steamed clams. Great food at really great prices.

CHEF MICHAEL'S
81671 Overseas Hwy, Islamorada, 305-664-0640
http://www.foodtotalkabout.com
CUISINE: Seafood / Vegetarian / Vegan
DRINKS: Beer & wine
SERVING: Dinner nightly, Sunday Brunch
PRICE RANGE: $$$
There are a lot of pathetically crappy restaurants in the Middle and Lower Keys (does the beer have to be that bad in so many places? Or the conch fritters heavy with batter and low on conch?), but this isn't one of them. This upscale eatery offers Chef Michael's creative menu

of seafood & New American entrees close enough to the **Cheeca Lodge** that you can walk over. The dining room is small and intimate, seating under 30, but there's room for that many more outside on the porch. Menu picks include Hogfish (a specialty) and their infamous French toast for Sunday brunch. Great fish selections chosen from whatever local fishermen bring the chef that day, so you might get yellowtail, swordfish, grouper, tripletail, tuna—whatever they bring—and get it served either sautéed, grilled, blackened or fried. Dessert standouts are the really fine Key Lime Pie and the crème brulee made daily.

GILBERT'S RESORT TIKI BAR
107900 Overseas Hwy., Key Largo: 305-451-1133
gilbertsresort.com
CUISINE: German, Seafood
DRINKS: Full bar
SERVING: Daily lunch and dinner
PRICE RANGE: $$
This is perhaps the very first place in the Keys where you can experience that special laid-back feeling that people associate with the Keys. Barely anybody knows about it. Just a bit south of Homestead, just when you go into the Keys on Key Largo, you take the first right and you'll find yourself here at Gilbert's. If you see a sunset here, and you've never been to the Keys before, you'll want to continue south. Only 45 minutes from Miami (without traffic). Chef Georg Schu is from Germany, and this is the only place I know down here that serves German specialties (as well as local seafood).

GREEN TURTLE INN
81219 Overseas Hwy. at MM 81.2, Islamorada: 305-664-2006
www.greenturtleinn.com/
CUISINE: Seafood
DRINKS: Full Bar
SERVING: Breakfast/ Lunch/ Dinner
PRICE RANGE: $$$
Great little eatery that offers a gourmet market and dishes cooked with locally farmed produce and microgreens. For lunch they have an excellent fried green tomato BLT and at breakfast, their coconut French toast is a must. Check out the art gallery and gourmet shop.

HARRIETTE'S RESTAURANT
95710 Overseas Hwy. at MM 95.7, Key Largo: 305-852-8689
https://www.facebook.com/HarriettesRestaurant
CUISINE: Breakfast/ Brunch
DRINKS: No alcohol
SERVING: Breakfast

PRICE RANGE: $
Open only for breakfast (until 2 pm) this place packs in a major crowd. On a diet? No problem. Aside from their enormous homemade biscuits and muffins, this place offers a South Beach Diet and Atkins diet menu. (But I've never had any of the diet foods—the breakfasts are too good, especially the hash browns.)

HUNGRY TARPON
77522 Overseas Hwy, Islamorada, 305-664-0535
www.hungrytarpon.com
CUISINE: Seafood / Caribbean
DRINKS: Full Bar
SERVING: Lunch & Dinner
PRICE RANGE: $$
Casual seafood shack with a bayside deck—just what everybody's image is of a little waterfront eatery in the Keys. They have a great blackened grouper sandwich. Great food offerings but you can also bring your own catch to be cooked by the chef. Restaurant is surrounded by artisan kiosks and a bait and tackle shop.

ISLAMORADA FISH COMPANY
81532 Overseas Hwy. at MM 81.5, Islamorada: 305-664-9271
http://www.islamoradafishco.com
CUISINE: Seafood
DRINKS: Full Bar
SERVING: Breakfast/ Lunch/ Dinner
PRICE RANGE: $
Don't let its average looks fool you, this place is serving up some incredible dishes including outstanding breakfasts. Keep your eyes on the water; manatees are known to drift by.

ISLAND GRILL
85501 Overseas Hwy. at MM 85, Islamorada: 305-664-8400
http://keysislandgrill.com
CUISINE: Seafood
DRINKS: Full Bar
SERVING: Breakfast/ Lunch/ Dinner
PRICE RANGE: $
Located just under the Snake Creek Bridge, this place has a sprawling outdoor deck and bar with intimate waterfront dining. Serving up fresh fish, shrimp and calamari; you can also bring your own catch and they will cook it up for you.

KAIYO GRILL & SUSHI
81701 Old Hwy. at MM 82, Islamorada: 305-664-5556

http://www.kaiyokeys.com
CUISINE: Japanese/ Sushi
DRINKS: Wine/ Sake
SERVING: Lunch/ Dinner
PRICE RANGE: $$$$
This eclectic, colorful restaurant looks completely out of place in the Keys but with their superb, contemporary sushi, people from all over South Florida are finding their way here. Although diners are casually dressed, the service is a notch above.

KEY LARGO CONCH HOUSE RESTAURANT & COFFEE BAR
100211 Overseas Hwy. at MM 100, Key Largo: 305-453-4844
www.keylargoconchhouse.com
CUISINE: American
DRINKS: Full Bar
SERVING: Breakfast/ Lunch/ Dinner
PRICE RANGE: $
Featured on the Food Network, the Conch House is exactly that, a house set amidst lush landscaping with great food priced right. A local hotspot, this is a pet friendly eatery. This family-owned spot is a favorite among locals for the quality of its conch fritters, and they even host an annual Conch Fritter Eating Contest awarding laurels to whoever eats the most of them in 10 minutes. But to rush is an anomaly in the Keys—sit on the large veranda and relax.

KEYS FISHERIES MARKET & MARINA
3502 Gulfview Ave., Marathon: 305-743-4353
keysfisheries.com
CUISINE: Seafood
DRINKS: Full bar
SERVING: Daily lunch and dinner
PRICE RANGE: $$
Not only a marina, but a fish market and a restaurant, too. Similar to those places you see up on Cape Cod where you know the fish is fresh because you can see it in the display case. Lobster Reuben, blackened mahi mahi, fried conch and get a blooming onion. (If you catch your own fish, they'll cook it up for you.)

LAZY DAYS
79867 Overseas Hwy. at MM 79.9, Islamorada: 305-664-5256
http://www.lazydaysrestaurant.com
CUISINE: Seafood/ Bar fare
DRINKS: Full Bar
SERVING: Lunch/ Dinner
PRICE RANGE: $$

As the name implies, this oceanfront eatery is very laid back. Here you'll find outstanding fresh seafood and if you like, the chef will even cook up your own catch. Great happy hour from 4-6 pm.

LORELEI RESTAURANT AND CABANA BAR
81924 Overseas Hwy, Islamorada: 305-664-2692
http://www.loreleicabanabar.com/
CUISINE: Seafood/ Bar fare
DRINKS: Full Bar
SERVING: Breakfast/ Lunch/ Dinner
PRICE RANGE: $$
Big old fish house and bar with great views of the gulf, this is a great place for simple seafood. Great dishes are served up with live music in the evenings.

MARKER 88
88000 Overseas Hwy. at MM 88, Islamorada: 305-852-9315
http://www.marker88.info
CUISINE: Seafood

DRINKS: Full Bar
SERVING: Dinner
PRICE RANGE: $$$
Everything served up here is grown and caught locally. Service might be a little slow but the views and the food are worth it. This is one of those places that makes a great stop when you're driving down to Key West. It's also one of those places where you'll want to propose to whoever you're with, but be careful when gazing into that gorgeous sunset. As nice as Marker 88 is, you can still dress in jeans and flip-flops and not feel out of place.

PIERRE'S
81600 Overseas Hwy. at MM 81.6, Islamorada: 305-664-3225
www.moradabay.com/pierres
CUISINE: French
DRINKS: Full Bar
SERVING: Dinner
PRICE RANGE: $$$$
The décor of this restaurant does not match its cuisine, but that's not a bad thing. Moroccan, African and Indian objets d'art. French food will definitely impress. Dim lights and candlelight offer a unique experience. Want romance? Try the second floor veranda overlooking tiki torches and the ocean.

SNAPPER'S
139 Seaside Ave. at MM 94.5, Key Largo: 305-852-5956
http://www.snapperskeylargo.com
CUISINE: Seafood
DRINKS: Full Bar
SERVING: Lunch/ Dinner
PRICE RANGE: $
A local favorite, this place offers nightly live music for a very casual crowd. Kids love feeding the tarpon off the dock and if you wish, you may fish right there and they will cook up your catch. Free WiFi.

ZIGGIE AND MAD DOG'S
83000 Overseas Hwy., Islamorada: 305-664-3391
http://www.ziggieandmaddogs.com
CUISINE: Steakhouse
DRINKS: Full Bar
SERVING: Dinner
PRICE RANGE: $$$
This casually elegant eatery is friendly and fun. Owned by former Miami Dolphins player Jim Mandich, don't be surprised if you run into Mandich's famous athlete friends.

RESTAURANTS LOWER KEYS

COCO'S KITCHEN
283 Key Deer Blvd., Big Pine Key: 305-872-4495
http://www.cocoskitchen.com
CUISINE: Cuban/ International
DRINKS: No alcohol
SERVING: Breakfast/ Lunch/ Dinner
PRICE RANGE: $
Don't let the shopping plaza location fool you, this place serves up everything from black beans and rice to several pasta dishes. Good food at great prices.

MANGROVE MAMA'S RESTAURANT
19991 Overseas Hwy, Sugarloaf Key: 305-745-3030
http://www.mangrovemamasrestaurant.com
CUISINE: Seafood/ Caribbean
DRINKS: Full Bar
SERVING: Brunch/ Lunch/ Dinner
PRICE RANGE: $$
This place has a true Keys ambiance. Simple tables shaded by banana trees and palm fronds. They serve the beer in jelly glasses. Although fish is what's mostly on the menu, you can also have soups, salads and sandwiches. Check out the miniature horses out back.

NO NAME PUB
30813 N Watson Blvd, 1/4 mile south of No Name Bridge, Big Pine Key: 305-872-9115
http://www.nonamepub.com
CUISINE: Pub fare/ Pizza
DRINKS: Full Bar
SERVING: Lunch/ Dinner
PRICE RANGE: $
Funky, old bar in the middle of nowhere. Serves great pizza and subs. Check out their '80s tunes in the old jukebox.

RESTAURANTS KEY WEST

ALONZO & BERLIN'S LOBSTER HOUSE
A&B LOBSTER HOUSE
700 Front St., Key West: 305-294-5880
http://aandblobsterhouse.com
CUISINE: Seafood
DRINKS: Full Bar
SERVING: Dinner
PRICE RANGE: $$$$
Overall a good restaurant with good food. Seating on the outside offers a beautiful view of the marina. Service is good but can sometimes be a bit rushed.

AMBROSIA
1401 Simonton St., Key West: 305-293-0304
http://ambrosiasushi.com/
CUISINE: Sushi
DRINKS: Beer/ Wine
SERVING: Lunch/ Dinner
PRICE RANGE: $
Undoubtedly the best sushi restaurant on the island, this eatery is tucked away in a resort near the beach.

ANTONIA'S
615 Duval St., Key West: 305-294-6565
http://www.antoniaskeywest.com
CUISINE: Italian
DRINKS: Full Bar
SERVING: Dinner
PRICE RANGE: $$$
Great place for the traditional Italian favorites. Pastas are homemade and the ambience is quaint and cozy.

AZUR
425 Grinnell St., Key West: 305-292-2987
www.azurkeywest.com
CUISINE: American (New), Mediterranean
DRINKS: Beer & Wine
SERVING: Breakfast, Lunch & Dinner.
PRICE RANGE: $$
Dine in a beautiful blue dining room or on a shaded terrace. This restaurant serves a delicious selection of Mediterranean specialties. Great seafood, atmosphere, and service.

BAD BOY BURRITO
1128 Simonton St., Key West: 305-292-2697
http://www.badboyburrito.com
CUISINE: Mexican
DRINKS: No alcohol
SERVING: Lunch/ Dinner
PRICE RANGE: $
Great burritos and great tacos, not many places to sit so take-out is probably best. Closes 10pm.

BAGATELLE
115 Duval St., Key West: 305-296-6609
http://www.bagatellekeywest.com
CUISINE: Seafood, Tropical
DRINKS: Full Bar
SERVING: Lunch/ Dinner
PRICE RANGE: $$$
Take a seat on the second-floor veranda and you will have a great view for people watching on ever-busy Duval Street. All the dishes here, including chicken and beef, are given the tropical treatment.

BANANA CAFÉ
1215 Duval St., Key West: 305-294-7227
www.bananacafekw.com
CUISINE: French
DRINKS: Beer/ Wine
SERVING: Breakfast/ Lunch/ Dinner
PRICE RANGE: $$
This Country French local café has a strong, loyal clientele. Great food at affordable prices. Live jazz on Thursday nights.

BLUE HEAVEN
729 Thomas St., Key West: 305-296-8666
http://www.blueheavenkw.com WEBSITE DOWN AT PRESSTIME

CUISINE: Seafood, American
DRINKS: Full Bar
SERVING: Breakfast/ Lunch/ Dinner
PRICE RANGE: $$

You can't get more "Key West" than this hippie-run restaurant that has some of the best food in town. Be prepared to wait in line. Don't let the dirty floors and roaming cats and birds put you off; give this place a shot. They say Hemingway (a big boxing fan) used to referee matches here every Friday night.

B.O.'S FISH WAGON
801 Caroline St., Key West: 305-294-9272
bosfishwagon.com
CUISINE: Seafood
DRINKS: Beer / Wine
SERVING: Daily lunch and dinner
PRICE RANGE: $$

You can't get more Keys lifestyle than this—there's nothing more to this dump than a tawdry little shack where the walls are covered with old rusty license plates, fishnets, sponges, buoys that have seen better days. (Some of the customers have seen better days, too.) There's even a rusted out old truck outside. But who cares? People have a great time here. The menu is limited, mainly to fried fish sandwiches (grouper, daily catch, soft shell crab, shrimp or cracked conch) and a very good chili dog, but the standout here would be the conch fritters. Somebody's always pounding away on the piano and after a while people get up and start dancing.

THE CAFÉ, A MOSTLY VEGETARIAN PLACE
509 Southard St., Key West: 305-296-5515
www.thecafekw.com
CUISINE: Vegetarian
DRINKS: Beer/ Wine
SERVING: Lunch/ Dinner
PRICE RANGE: $

Not a vegetarian? Neither am I, but this place proves you don't have to be in order to enjoy the great food. Favorites include homemade soups and veggie burgers. Their Sunday brunch is worth checking out.

CAFÉ MARQUESA
600 Fleming St., Key West: 305-292-1919
http://www.marquesa.com
CUISINE: Contemporary American
DRINKS: Full Bar
SERVING: Dinner

PRICE RANGE: $$$$
Intimate, cozy restaurant with amazing food and fantastic service. They close for two weeks during summer so call ahead. Reservations are suggested.

CAFÉ SOLÉ
1029 Southard St., Key West: 305-294-0230
http://www.cafesole.com
CUISINE: French
DRINKS: Wine/ Beer
SERVING: Dinner
PRICE RANGE: $$$
Great place to find a taste of France, tucked away in a residential neighborhood. Mutton snapper in wine is great and the bouillabaisse is pretty damned good. Latticework against the walls gives this place the kind of Key West ambiance you come down here to experience. Cozy, intimate, charming.

COMMODORE WATERFRONT
700 Front St., Key West: 305-294-9191
www.commodorekeywest.com
CUISINE: Steakhouse
DRINKS: Full Bar
SERVING: Dinner
PRICE RANGE: $$$
Two levels of dining, downstairs is the Boathouse and upstairs is the Commodore, offering excellent selection of steaks and seafood. Warm atmosphere, great service.

CONCH REPUBLIC SEAFOOD CO.
631 Greene St., Key West: 305-294-4403
www.conchrepublicseafood.com

CUISINE: Seafood
DRINKS: Full Bar
SERVING: Lunch, Dinner
PRICE RANGE: $$
An open-air restaurant overlooking the historic seaport and the Key West Marina. Waterfront dining with a menu that features Caribbean influenced cuisine and of course great seafood. Live music, good service.

CROISSANTS DE FRANCE
816 Duval St., Key West: 305-294-2624
www.croissantsdefrance.com
CUISINE: Bakery, French Café
DRINKS: Beer & Wine
SERVING: Breakfast, Lunch, Dinner
PRICE RANGE: $$
Bistro on one side, bakery on the other. Great fresh baked croissants, delicious crepes, pastries, soups and sandwiches. Patio dining.

CUBAN COFFEE QUEEN
284 Margaret St, Key West, 305-292-4747
www.cubancoffeequeen.com
CUISINE: Cuban/Breakfast
DRINKS: No Booze
SERVING: Breakfast, Lunch & Dinner
PRICE RANGE: $
Popular Cuban counter-serve spot that offers great Cuban coffee drinks and traditional Cuban fare. Daily specials.

DJ'S CLAM SHACK
629 Duval St., Key West: 305-294-0102
http://www.djsclamshack.com
CUISINE: American/ Seafood
DRINKS: Beer/ Wine
SERVING: Lunch/ Dinner
PRICE RANGE: $
Not fancy, just awesome! Informal eating at its best, you will be blown away by their lobster roll, clams and conch fritters. Friendly service and budget friendly.

DUFFY'S STEAK & LOBSTER HOUSE
1007 Simonton St., Key West: 305-296-4900
www.duffyskeywest.com
CUISINE: Steakhouse, Seafood
DRINKS: Full Bar
SERVING: Dinner
PRICE RANGE: $$$
Italian steak and lobster house offering a menu that includes a variety of seafood including dolphin. A locals favorite. Good food, good service.

FIRST FLIGHT ISLAND RESTAURANT & BREWERY
301 Whitehead St, Key West, 305-293-8484
www.firstflightkw.com
CUISINE: American (New)
DRINKS: Full Bar
SERVING: Lunch, dinner; one of the best happy hours in town
PRICE RANGE: $$
Located in the former location of Kelly's Caribbean Bar, this newly decorated venue offers a casual eatery serving American fare. Creative cocktails. Brewery with 3 of their own brews on tap. Live music some nights.

FIVE BROTHERS GROCERY AND SANDWICH SHOP
930 Southard St (at Grinnell), Key West, 305-296-5205
CUISINE: Grocery / Cuban
DRINKS: No Booze
SERVING: Daily 6-6; closed Sun
PRICE RANGE: $
Next to a very downmarket laundromat is the popular grocery and sandwich shop combination that is a favorite of locals and tourists. Run by a Cuban, so the food is good food and so is the café con leche. Munch on guava pastries and ham croquettes. There's a really lip-smacking breakfast sandwich with ham, eggs and cheese on Cuban

bread pressed thin. BBQ Pork Sandwich and the Fried Grouper sandwich.

FRENCHIE'S CAFÉ
529 United St., Key West: 305-900-396-7124
www.frenchieskeywest.com
CUISINE: French, Café
DRINKS: No Alcohol
SERVING: Breakfast, Lunch
PRICE RANGE: $
Great inexpensive place for breakfast or lunch. Delicious, fresh sandwiches. Great coffee. Friendly service.

GLAZED DONUTS
420 Eaton St, Key West, 305-294-9142
www.glazeddonuts.com
CUISINE: Donuts / Cafe
DRINKS: No Booze
SERVING: Breakfast & Lunch
PRICE RANGE: $$
Not your typical donut shop, these are the ultimate deluxe donuts – key lime custard cream and chocolate covered are the best. All donuts made from scratch.

HALF SHELL RAW BAR
231 Margaret St, Key West, 305-294-7496
www.halfshellrawbar.com
CUISINE: Seafood
DRINKS: Full Bar
SERVING: Lunch & Dinner
PRICE RANGE: $$
Set in a former shrimp-packing facility, this casual fish shack features waterside seating on picnic tables. The décor is pretty minimalistic—lots of license plates from all over the world are nailed to the walls. At twilight you'll be able to watch as boats leave the marina for their "sunset cruises." Happy hour brings ridiculous low prices for beers and oysters on the half shell. Menu includes: Gulf oysters, stuffed shrimp, and stuffed snapper. Hang out and enjoy the shuffleboard tables.

HOT TIN ROOF
Ocean Key Resort & Spa
0 Duval St., Key West: 305-296-7701
http://www.oceankey.com/key-west-restaurant
CUISINE: International Fusion
DRINKS: Full Bar

SERVING: Dinner
PRICE RANGE: $$$$
Offering indoor and outdoor deck seating overlooking the harbor, this restaurant is the epitome of casual elegance. Here, the menu is a bit of a mixed bag, with French, Asian and South American specialties. Reserve ahead in season.

ISLAND DOGS BAR
505 Front St., Key West: 305-509-7136
http://www.islanddogsbar.com
CUISINE: American
DRINKS: Full Bar
SERVING: Lunch/ Dinner
PRICE RANGE: $
Not what you would typically expect from bar food, this place has delicious burgers, chicken fingers and chicken wings. Great people watching.

LA TE DA
1125 Duval St., Key West: 305-296-6706
lateda.com
CUISINE: American
DRINKS: Full bar
SERVING: Lunch, dinner
PRICE RANGE: $$$
Super place for lunch or dinner. The atmosphere is just great, eating outside under the trees by the pool. Or on the balcony. Omelet cake with pancetta, fontina cheese, arugula, oven roasted tomatoes and spinach, oysters remoulade and scallops wrapped in Serano ham, rosemary and mustard-crusted pork tenderloin, tamarind-glazed lamb loin and garlic shrimp served over polenta. Yum.

LA TRATTORIA
524 Duval St., Key West: 305-296-1075
http://www.latrattoria.us
CUISINE: Italian
DRINKS: Full Bar
SERVING: Dinner
PRICE RANGE: $$$
True traditional Italian dishes served in a relaxed atmosphere. Staff is very friendly. Stop by their cocktail lounge, Virgilio's, for live jazz until 2am.

LATITUDES BEACH CAFÉ
245 Front St., Key West: 305-292-5300
www.sunsetkeycottages.com
CUISINE: Caribbean, Seafood, Mexican
DRINKS: Full Bar
SERVING: Breakfast/ Lunch/ Dinner
PRICE RANGE: $$$$
Very nice atmosphere in this scenic restaurant. The food is good and the service is friendly. Try sitting at the bar at sunset for a wow factor.

LOUIE'S BACKYARD
700 Waddell Ave., Key West: 305-294-1061
http://www.louiesbackyard.com
CUISINE: Caribbean
DRINKS: Full Bar
SERVING: Lunch/ Dinner
PRICE RANGE: $$$$
Truly one of the most romantic restaurants around, the fact that it's located off the beaten path just lends to the charm. Dishes are the creation of famed Chef Norman Van Aken, sunset cocktails are ideal at the oceanfront tiki bar. Reserve ahead.

MANGIA, MANGIA
900 Southard St., Key West: 305-294-2469
http://www.mangia-mangia.com
CUISINE: Italian
DRINKS: Beer/ Wine
SERVING: Dinner
PRICE RANGE: $$

Off the beaten path, this place serves up homemade pastas and tasty marinara sauce. Relax out back in their charming patio with a glass of wine or a beer from their rather large selection.

MANGOES
700 Duval St., Key West: 305-294-8002
www.mangoeskeywest.com/
CUISINE: American, Seafood
DRINKS: Beer/ Wine
SERVING: Lunch/ Dinner/ Late night
PRICE RANGE: $$$
The brick patio shaded by the canopy of large banyan trees makes this place packed almost every day. Even though it's located on touristy Duval Street, check out the back bar for a locals loungy scene.

MARTIN'S
917 Duval St., Key West: 305-295-0111
http://www.martinskeywest.com
CUISINE: American/German
DRINKS: Full Bar
SERVING: Dinner/ Sunday brunch
PRICE RANGE: $$$$
Very elegant dining in a contemporary setting. Indoor/outdoor. Has some German specialties like Duck Breast "Schwarzwald" (grilled duck breast served in a Burgundy sauce, with red cabbage and rosemary potatoes, garnished with a poached pear half & Lingonberry marmalade and Jäger Schnitzel (Wiener Schnitzel topped with a mushroom sauce and served with Spätzle. But I end up going for the lamb osso bucco. Also excellent seafood and pasta dishes. And here you can get Maine lobster, a welcome relief from the ubiquitous Florida variety. Apple strudel for dessert is a must.

MATTHEESSEN'S 4TH OF JULY ICE CREAM PARLOR
419 Duval St & 106 Duval St, Key West, 305-923-5418

http://mattskeywest.com/
CUISINE: American/ Desserts
DRINKS: No alcohol
SERVING: Lunch/ Dinner
PRICE RANGE: $

For junk food junkies. Serving up humongous portions of ice cream (one is enough to share) and incredible monster cookies, this place also offers great hamburgers and fries, grilled cheese sandwiches, onion rings and club wraps.

MICHAEL'S RESTAURANT
532 Margaret St., Key West: 305-295-1300
http://www.michaelskeywest.com WEBSITE DOWN AT PRESSTIME
CUISINE: American
DRINKS: Full Bar
SERVING: Dinner
PRICE RANGE: $$$

Great selection of dishes, from steak to veal to duck. Prime steaks come in from Allen Brothers in Chicago. Seafood is excellent, but try the seared duck in the port wine demi-glace. Remember fondues? Never see those anymore, right? They serve several types here: beer & cheese (they use a strong Wisconsin cheddar in this one), wild mushroom, a "pesto pot" and the classic Gruyere cheese version. Indoor-outdoor.

MR Z'S
501 Southard St., Key Wes: 305-296-4445
http://www.mrzskeywest.com
CUISINE: American
DRINKS: Beer/ Wine
SERVING: Lunch/ Dinner/ Late night
PRICE RANGE: $

Great pizza, great cheesesteak sandwich but terrible service and even worse is their delivery.

NINE ONE FIVE BISTRO & WINE BAR
915 Duval St., Key West: 305-296-0669
www.915duval.com
CUISINE: American, Seafood
DRINKS: Full Bar
SERVING: Dinner
PRICE RANGE: $$$
Great place for watching the sunset on the porch. Excellent service and great food choices like the filet mignon beef carpaccio and stone crab.

ONLYWOOD PIZZERIA TRATTORIA
613 ½ Duval St. (in rear), Key West: 305-735-4412
www.onlywoodkw.com
CUISINE: Italian
DRINKS: Beer / Wine
SERVING: Daily lunch and dinner
PRICE RANGE: $$
Tucked between (and behind) 2 buildings off frenetic Duval Street is this completely delightful "find" where you can smell oregano and basil growing in the garden. The pizza here is cooked in a wood-burning oven sent over from Naples. Locals come here for the excellent pizza. They make their own mozzarella, which is understandably featured on many of their pies along with items such an anchovies, sausage, etc. Seafood pizzas are very good: Key West shrimp, clams, calamari, scallops.

PANINI PANINI
1075 Duval St., Key West: 305-296-2002
http://www.paninikw.com
CUISINE: Sandwiches/ Vegetarian/ Smoothies
DRINKS: Beer/ Wine
SERVING: Breakfast/ Lunch/ Dinner
PRICE RANGE: $
The food is really good and very reasonably priced. Fresh baked bread and a great selection of drinks and smoothies. Friendly staff.

PEPE'S
806 Caroline St., Key West: 305-294-7192
http://pepescafe.net WEBSITE DOWN AT PRESSTIME
CUISINE: American
DRINKS: Full Bar
SERVING: Breakfast/ Lunch/ Dinner
PRICE RANGE: $$

Good, basic food includes steak, oysters, chili, fish sandwiches and burgers. You will enjoy this rustic eatery with historical Key West photos on the walls.

SANDY'S CAFÉ
1026 White St., Key West: 305-296-4747
http://sandyscafe.com/
CUISINE: Cuban; Seafood; Deli
DRINKS: No booze
SERVING: Open 24 hours
PRICE RANGE: $
When you see the sign reading M&M Laundry, you know you're there. It's just a little take-out window, but if you hanker for an honest-to-God Cuban sandwich (ham, pork, lettuce and pickles—get extra mustard), this is the place in Key West to get it. You'll commonly see police and fire rescue personnel here at all hours. Why? It's good. And it's cheap.

SANTIAGO'S BODEGA
207 Petronia St., Suite 101, Key West: 305-296-7691
http://www.santiagosbodega.com
CUISINE: Tapas/ Small Plates
DRINKS: Beer/ Wine
SERVING: Lunch/ Dinner
PRICE RANGE: $$$
Off the beaten path and away from the crowds, this great eatery is located in the Bahama Village. Excellent selection of small dishes and both hot and cold tapas like smoked salmon carpaccio with crostini, crème fraiche, capers, and minced onions, tomato and basil bruschetta with olive tapenade on crostini, yellowfin ceviche, marinated in spicy citrus juice and served with avocado, mango, and cilantro, the trio (traditional hummus, roasted red pepper hummus, and black olive tapenade) served with pita bread, Roman meatballs in a nest of angel hair pasta, pinchos morunos, spicy marinated skewers of pork tenderloin with apple-mango chutney, beef tenderloin, seared and

topped with bleu cheese butter, croquettas, cayenne spiced pan-fried patties of potatoes, house ground prosciutto and provolone cheese with scallion cream, lamb patties, ground leg of lamb, fresh thyme, sherry, and lemon zest with a cucumber and feta salad. Their sangria is a must have.

SARABETH'S
530 Simonton St., Key West: 305-293-8181
http://sarabethskeywest.com
CUISINE: American
DRINKS: Full Bar
SERVING: Breakfast/ Lunch/ Dinner
PRICE RANGE: $$
An offshoot of the famed New York City hotspot, here you will find delicious breakfasts with their homemade jams and jellies. For lunch and dinner, you will find everything from Caesar salad to burgers to chicken pot pie.

SEVEN FISH
Truman Ave., Key West: 305-296-2777
http://www.7fish.com
CUISINE: Seafood
DRINKS: Full Bar
SERVING: Dinner
PRICE RANGE: $$$
Favorite seafood restaurant amongst locals: "simple, good food" is their motto.

SOUTHERNMOST BEACH CAFE
1405 Duval St., Key West: 305-295-6550
http://www.southernmostbeachcafe.com
CUISINE: American
DRINKS: Full Bar
SERVING: Breakfast/ Lunch/ Dinner
PRICE RANGE: $
Incredible views, incredible food and incredible prices. This place has a great cheap breakfast. Service might be a little slow. Great happy hour specials.

TAVERN N TOWN
3841 N. Roosevelt Blvd., Key West: 305-296-8100
www.tavernntown.com
CUISINE: Floribbean/ International
DRINKS: Full Bar
SERVING: Lunch/ Dinner

PRICE RANGE: $$$$
Another creation of famed chef Norman Van Aken, here you will find everything from seafood and steak to vegetable pad Thai. There is also a selection of tapas and small plates.

THAI CUISINE
513 Greene St., Key West: 305-294-9424
www.keywestthaicuisine.com WEBSITE DOWN AT PRESSTIME
CUISINE: Thai
DRINKS: Full Bar
SERVING: Lunch & Dinner
PRICE RANGE: $$
Thai cuisine and sushi with variety of vegetarian options. Service not great but the good is good. Off the beaten path location.

TURTLE KRAALS RESTAURANT & BAR
231 Margaret St., Key West: 305-294-2640
http://www.turtlekraals.com
CUISINE: Southwestern/ Seafood
DRINKS: Full Bar
SERVING: Lunch/ Dinner
PRICE RANGE: $$
This converted warehouse with indoor and dockside seating has something for everyone. Kids will especially like the wildlife exhibits that include a turtle cannery.

WHITE STREET SANDWICH SHOP
1222 White St, Key West, 305-797-6871
www.thebestcoffeeintown.net
CUISINE: Cuban / Deli
DRINKS: No Booze
SERVING: 5 a.m. – 6 p.m. daily

PRICE RANGE: $
Right in the heart of the Key West seaport, this street shop sells great Cuban sandwiches, superior Cuban coffee and an excellent mound of pulled pork with rice & beans.

Chapter 4
NIGHTLIFE

UPPER & MIDDLE KEYS

Nightlife in the Keys pretty much translates into the word: "bar." There just ain't nothin' else to do. There's no theatre, no culture of any kind (except for some hit or miss things in Key West).

HOG HEAVEN
85361 Overseas Hwy. at MM 85.3, Islamorada: 305-664-9669
http://www.hogheavensportsbar.com
This waterside biker bar has big screen TVs, video games and pool tables. Most patrons are regulars. Open daily from 11am to 4am.

TIKI BAR AT THE HOLIDAY ISLE RESORT
84001 Overseas Hwy. at MM 84, Islamorada: 305-664-2321
http://www.holidayisle.com
This place offers booze, dancing and a great time practically at any time of the day. Equal mix of tourists and locals.

WOODY'S SALOON AND RESTAURANT
81908 Overseas Hwy. at MM 82, Islamorada: 305-664-4335
http://www.woodysinthekeys.com
Wacky, loud and raunchy; this place is not for the faint of heart. With buck-naked strippers and a live band, this place also has a show that highlights a 300 pound native American who does a rude and crude routine of politically incorrect jokes. You've been warned.

NIGHTLIFE KEY WEST

AQUA
711 Duval St., Key West: 305-294-0555
http://www.aquakeywest.com
Very friendly gay bar, this place welcomes everybody. Don't be shy and step inside, you will love their drag shows. Great dance floor and great music in a very sociable environment.

BLUE MOJITO POOL BAR & GRILL
Hyatt Key West Resort and Spa
601 Front St., Key West, 305-809-1234
https://keywest.centric.hyatt.com
Enjoy cocktails overlooking the Gulf of Mexico in this sophisticated Key West bar. Great daily happy hour specials. Live music.

BOTTLECAP LOUNGE & LIQUOR STORE
1128 Simonton St., Key West: 305-296-2807
http://www.bottlecapkeywest.com

Great dive bar. This place has it all: Top DJs, live music, dance bar, music videos, lounge area, patio bar and pool tables. Some of the seating in the lounge area can be quite intimate, or at least as intimate as you can get in this kind of rowdy establishment.

BOURBON STREET PUB
724 Duval St., Key West: 305-294-9354
http://www.bourbonstreetpub.com
Techno and alternative music pumps out to a gay/straight mixed crowd. Great place to dance and people watch. There is also a pool and garden bar if you need a break from the dance floor.

CAPTAIN TONY'S SALOON
428 Greene St., Key West: 305-294-1838
http://www.capttonyssaloon.com
Once a morgue, this spirited bar is said to have been home to the original Sloppy Joe's, having entertained author Ernest Hemingway. Rustic and smoky, check out the "hanging tree" located inside the bar.

CORK & STOGIE CIGAR AND WINE BAR
1218 Duval St., Key West: 305-517-6419
www.corkandstogie.com
Friendly place to drink and smoke cigars if that's your thing. Small front porch for relaxing. Great wine selection.

COWBOY BILL'S HONKY TONK SALOON
618 Duval St., Key West: 305-292-1865
http://www.cowboybillskw.net/

A country-western sports bar with a mechanical bull. A rowdy crowd and lots of games including pool, darts, & video games. 27 TVs for watching sports. Live music.

D'VINE WINE GALLERY @ THE GARDENS HOTEL
526 Angela St., Key West: 305-294-2661
www.gardenshotel.com
A unique state-of-the-art wine tasting bar that offers up 32 bottles for sampling. Cabaret nights on Thursdays & Live Jazz in the Gardens on Sundays.

GARDEN OF EDEN
224 Duval St., Key West: 305-296-4565
www.bullkeywest.com/GARDENcoupon.asp
Two flights up on the side of the building, this bar is completely clothing optional. During the day, you will find sun worshippers vying for the perfect tan and at night, you will find a great mix of people (some of them opting for the no clothing alternative) enjoying the bird's eye view of the debauchery on Duval Street.

GRAND VIN WINE SHOP & BAR
1107 Duval St., Key West: 305-296-1020
A casual inviting wine shop and bar with a nice selection of wines. Hang out with the regulars or relax on the porch overlooking Duval Street.

GREEN PARROT BAR
601 Whitehead St., Key West: 305-294-6133
http://www.greenparrot.com

Green Parrot is more than a bar; it's a Key West icon. Known as an open-air hipster watering hole, there's live music on most nights. Locals' hangout. Legend has it Hemingway used to stop here on his walk home after leaving Sloppy Joe's. (And it looks like they haven't changed anything since.)

HOG'S BREATH SALOON
400 Front St., Key West: 305-296-4222
http://www.hogsbreath.com
This place is right across the street form Mallory Square, ground zero for sunset festivities. Live entertainment goes on daily, as well as the raucous partying. Friendly staff.

LA TE DA
La Te Da Hotel, 1125 Duval St., Key West: 305-296-6706
http://www.lateda.com
Located in the La Te Da Hotel, with three great bars, the outside Terrace Bar, the inside Piano Bar, and the upstairs Crystal Bar. Has a popular drag revue. Tourists and locals frequent these gay establishments (you don't have to be gay to enjoy the shows). The sheer gorgeousness of this place overshadows the excellent food they turn out.

RICK'S & DURTY HARRY'S
202 Duval St., Key West: 305-296-5513
www.ricksanddurtyharrys.com
Complex with eight unique bars. Live music every night. Late night karaoke every night at midnight. Drink specials.

RUM BAR AT THE SPEAKEASY INN
1117 Duval St., Key West: 305-296-2680
www.speakeasyinn.com
Small hotel bar with a comfortable atmosphere. Very friendly. Great place to start the night.

SCHOONER WHARF BAR
202 William, Key West: 305-292-3302
www.schoonerwharf.com
A locals' favorite located on the water. Boat-like ambiance. Great seafood. Live music. Two happy hours.

SMOKIN' TUNA SALOON
4 Charles St., Key West: 305-517-6350
www.smokintunasaloon.com
Very friendly bar (crowd and bartender) with live music, fresh seafood & raw bar. Outdoor seating.

Chapter 5
ATTRACTIONS

UPPER & MIDDLE KEYS

I'm not sure if you're already familiar with the Everglades just above and to the west of the Keys, but if you haven't yet had the special experiences to be had in the 'Glades, I'll drop in some very basic information you can use to learn more.

EVERGLADES NATIONAL PARK
Shark Valley Visitor Center, 36000 SW Eighth St. (Hwy. 41, also called the Tamiami Trail) in West Miami-Dade County. 305-242-7700. http://www.nps.gov/ever/index.htm.
By all means, if you have time before you hit the Keys, look over this web site for a few minutes and maybe that will convince you to make a side trip.

BIG CYPRESS NATIONAL PRESERVE
Entrance is off I-75 (Alligator Alley) and Hwy. 41 (Tamiami Trail). There's a Big Cypress Welcome Center at 33100 Tamiami Trail, Ochopee, 239-695-2000. Also the Oasis Visitor Center, 52105 Tamiami Trail East, Ochopee, 239-695-1201. www.nps.gov/bicy.
I've often found the Big Cypress far more interesting than the 'Glades. It's really a scary kind of place where you feel like you're going back in time to a prehistoric era. (Not much has changed here in millions of years except for the depredations humankind has caused.)

In the Keys
There are several places in the Upper and Middle Keys where you have an unusual opportunity available in very few places to interact with marine and animal life. Check below for details.

AFRICAN QUEEN
Holiday Inn, US 1 at Mile Marker 100, Key Largo: 305-896-8004 or 305-451-8080. www.africanqueenflkeys.com. Offers 90-minute canal cruises and some dinner cruises. Rates vary.
This is the actual boat used in the famous John Huston-directed 1951 movie *African Queen*, starring Bogart and Hepburn. Restored at a cost of $60,000, it was originally named the S/L Livingstone (S/L stands for Steam Launch). It was built in 1912 and shipped to Uganda where it did service on the Ruiki River and Lake Albert, a body of water bordering the Belgian Congo. Departs from the Marina Del Mar and travels down the Port Largo Canals to the Atlantic Ocean before turning around to return.

BACKCOUNTRY COWBOY OUTFITTERS
82240 Overseas Hwy., Islamorada: 305-517-4177
www.backcountrycowboy.com

Kayaking, camping, everglades kayaking, bike rentals—lots of different things going on.

CRANE POINT HAMMOCK
5550 Overseas Hwy., Marathon: 305-743-9100
http://www.cranepoint.net
ADMISSION: varies
Full of rich botanical and archaeological history of the Keys, this nature area is considered one of the most important historic sites in the Keys. It contains the last virgin thatch-palm hammock in North America, a rainforest exhibit, and an archaeological site with prehistoric Indian and Bahamian artifacts.

DAGNY JOHNSON HAMMOCK BOTANICAL STATE PARK
Route 905, North Key Largo: 305-451-1202. www.stateparks.com
(This is 1 mile north of US 1.) In this park covering some 2400 acres, you can see what most of the Upper Keys looked like before humans moved in with the bulldozers. Tropical hardwood hammocks and mangrove wetlands are what I'm talking about. Over 100 rare plants and animals. Guided tours if you want them.

DOLPHIN RESEARCH CENTER
58901 Overseas Hwy., Grassy Key: 305-289-1121
Mile Marker 59
http://www.dolphins.org
ADMISSION: verify rates, as they may have changed.
Within a 90,000 square foot saltwater pool, you are allowed to interact with a family of 19 dolphins. These dolphins enjoy human interaction, they nuzzle and seem to smile and kiss the lucky people who get to interact with them in daily interactive programs. Or cozy up to a sea lion.

EVERGLADES ECO-TOURS
Dolphin's Cove, 101900 US 1, Key Largo: 305-394-7422
www.captainsterling.com.
Offers several tours. There's even one that takes you from Key Largo across the Everglades to Flamingo, the most remote point in Florida. (The boats hold no more than 6 people, so it's not crowded.) They also run short tours and sunset tours. Rates vary.

FISHING
There's a wide selection of private charter boats, or you can go out on a big boat. One of these ships is **SailorsChoice**, which you can board at the **Holiday Inn Docks**, 305-451-1802.
www.sailorschoicefishingboat.com. The boat is 65 feet and (thankfully for people like me) has an air-conditioned cabin.

FLORIDA KEYS OVERSEAS PADDLING TRAIL
For those truly intrepid paddlers, this is a "trail" that runs the whole 110-mile length of the Keys, beginning up here in Key Largo and running all the way down to Key West. It takes between 9 and 10 days if you do it all, but of course you can choose to do a small section of it

and get the idea. (The Atlantic route is longer than the Florida Bay route.) You can rent sea kayaks, canoes and all the gear you'll need at **Florida Bay Outfitters**, 104050 US 1, MM 104, 305-451-3018. www.kayakfloridakeys.com. This company also sets you up for single or multi-day paddle trips and has guided and other tour offerings.

FLORIDA KEYS BREWING CO.
200 Morada Way, Islamorada, 305-916-5206
www.floridakeysbrewingco.com
These people take brewing seriously. They serve island-themed beers brewed with top quality ingredients.

FLORIDA KEYS WILD BIRD CENTER
93600 Overseas Hwy., Tavernier: 305-852-4486
www.keepthemflying.org/
Feed the pelicans here. You'll see cages where injured peregrine falcons are rehabilitated. Great egrets and cormorants and in plentiful supply.

HISTORY OF DIVING MUSEUM
82990 Overseas Hwy, Islamorada, 305-664-9737
www.divingmuseum.org
HOURS: 10 – 5 DAILY
ADMISSION: Minimal admission fee
Museum dedicated to celebrating the History of Diving. Here you'll see an eclectic collection of artifacts, books, antiques, documents, photographs and exhibitions – all related to the history of diving. Bell helmets, armored diving suits. This place has the world's largest collection of such artifacts.

JACOBS AQUATIC CENTER
320 Laguna Ave., Key Largo: 305-453-7946.
www.jacobsaquaticcenter.org. MM 99.6. They have 3 swimming pools here. One of them has a waterfall, a pirate ship with waterslides going off the deck into the pool. Another is a lap pool 25 meters long.

JOHN PENNEKAMP CORAL REEF STATE PARK
102601 Overseas Hwy., Key Largo: 305-451-6300.
www.pennekamppark.com
This is just one of the most amazing places in the world. It's the first undersea park in the U.S., and you could easily spend a week here. (And many do!)

It's about the coral reefs and the multi-colored tropical fish that live around them that are the main attraction. Here, you will find fish (over 600 varieties in colors that will boggle your mind) and coral (over 40 kinds) in abundance, protected in a sanctuary that extends over 70 nautical square miles. This is the place for scuba and snorkeling experiences you won't find anywhere else in America. And what's also good is that scuba and snorkelers can mix easily, so if some members of your party aren't certified for scuba, you can all still go together.

At the Visitors' Center, there's a large aquarium where you can see some of the varieties of fish you'll later see when you go snorkeling and diving. (They rent all the equipment you'll need.)

You can rent powerboats and canoes and go out on your own, or you can take a guided trip out on the water. Glass-bottom boats, nature trails, and lots more.

When I was younger and did a lot of scuba, I once found myself in a school of barracuda down here. Thrilling. (But very scary.)

CAMPING: I'm not a camper. In fact, there's nothing I'd like to do less than go camping, but camping friends I have swear by this place. You'll find 47 full-facility sites for both tent and RV campers. Restrooms and hot showers are easily accessible. Call 1-800-326-3521.

CANOEING & KAYAKING
You can rent kayaks, "sea kayaks," canoes and powerboats from the **Coral Reef Park Company** (305-872-2353). Go for a few hours or a whole day, with or without a guide and explore the mangroves.

FISHING: Fishing is allowed only in designated areas in accordance with Florida law. Saltwater fishing licenses are required. Spearfishing and collecting of tropical fish is prohibited inside the park.

SWIMMING: Three areas are designated for swimming, including Canon Beach, which features remnants of an early Spanish shipwreck 100 feet offshore.

PICNICKING: Designated areas are located throughout the park. Barbeque grills are provided. No ground fires are permitted. To rent a pavilion, call 1-305-451-1202.

KEY LARGO BIKE AND ADVENTURE TOURS
90775 Old Hwy, Tavernier, 305-395-1551
www.keylargobike.com
Lots of different tours here if you want to know more about the Upper Keys. Rent and go on your own or take one of their tours: bike tours, hybrid bikes, cruiser bikes, stand-up paddleboards, historic 2-hour bike tour of Islamorada, and others.

MARATHON KAYAK
Marathon: 305-395-0355
www.marathonkayak.com
Guided kayak tours, mangrove tours, Everglades tours, bike/snorkel tours, family tours, day trips.

MICHELLE NICOLE LOWE ART GALLERY
81904 Overseas Hwy, Islamorada, 305-981-6424
www.michellenicolelowe.com
Gallery exhibiting the work of Key West artist Michelle Nicole Lowe – known for her paintings of tropical fish. Gallery offers a variety of paintings, prints, t-shirts and gift items.

M.V. KEY LARGO PRINCESS
99701 US 1, Key Largo: 305-451-4655
www.keylargoprincess.com.
From the dock at the Holiday Inn at MM 100, they have 3 departures daily on a 70-foot glass-bottom boat. Tour runs 2 hours. Rates vary.

ROBBIE'S OF ISLAMORADA
77522 Overseas Hwy, Islamorada, 305-664-8070
www.robbies.com
Explore the waters on the famous Captain Michael boat or one of the other vessels available for rent, snorkeling, fishing, or tours. Robbie's is surrounded by shopping, restaurants, and sidewalk vendors. Kayaks also available for rent.

THEATER OF THE SEA
U.S. 1 at MM 84.5, Islamorada: 305-664-2431
http://www.theaterofthesea.com
ADMISSION: varies
This is one of the oldest marine zoos, established in 1946. Book well in advance if you want to swim with the dolphins. Both the dolphin shows and the sea-lion shows are entertaining, especially for children.

TURTLE HOSPITAL
2396 Overseas Hwy., Marathon: 305-743-2552
turtlehospital.org
Wherever you live, you always read sentimental articles in the newspaper (or online) about people who rescue turtles. "Awww," you say. And so do I. Well, here in Marathon, you can actually visit a place where they care for turtles. What goes wrong with turtles? you might ask. A variety of turtle ailments are treated at the Turtle

Hospital including flipper amputations caused by fishing line and trap rope entanglements, shell damage caused by boat collisions, and intestinal impactions caused by ingestion of foreign materials such as plastic bags, balloons, and fishing line and/or hooks. The most common surgery performed is the removal of debilitating viral tumors that affect over 50% of the sea turtles in the Keys and around the world. This is a non-profit group, so after your visit, leave a donation.

WHEELS-2-GO
5994 Overseas Hwy., Marathon: 305-289-4279
www.wheels-2-go.com
Bikes and kayaks for rent.

ATTRACTIONS LOWER KEYS

BAHIA HONDA STATE PARK
36850 Overseas Hwy, Big Pine Key, 305-872-3210
http://www.bahiahondapark.com
Admission fee.
Great place for hiking, bird-watching, swimming, snorkeling, and fishing. Shaded seaside picnic areas contain tables and grills. With a narrow beach, this is one of the best beaches in the Lower Keys. Also, there's a historic railroad bridge that creeps out almost a mile that's been converted to a pedestrian pier. It was part of Henry Flagler's grand 1912 push to extend his railroad to Key West from Miami that got washed away in the Cat 5 hurricane of 1935. There's a snorkeling tour to **Looe Key Sanctuary Preservation Area** that leaves from here.

BIG PINE KAYAK ADVENTURES
The Old Wooden Bridge Fishing Camp, 1791 Bogie Dr., Big Pine Key: 305-872-7474
keyskayaktours.com
The boss here, Bill Keogh, specializes in Lower Florida Keys backcountry tours such as Half and Full Day Kayaking Nature Tours; Shallow-water Skiff Eco-tours; Short and Long Term Kayak Rentals; Backcountry Sailing Catamaran Cruises; Shallow-water Fishing.

FANTASY DAN AIR TOURS
Sugarloaf Key Airport, 16855 US 1, MM 17, Sugarloaf Key: 305-745-2217
Wide variety of flying tours available. Rates vary.

FLORIDA KEYS SEA SALT
Sugarloaf Key: 305-797-4977
www.floridakeysseasalt.com WEBSITE DOWN AT PRESSTIME
In the early 1800s, harvesting sea salt was a big moneymaker in these parts (also in the Carolinas). Along the eastern side of Key West, natural saltpans were everywhere. Bahamian workers were brought in because they knew how to do it. Now that's all gone, except for this little place. This isn't really a touristy stop, and I ought to put this listing in SHOPPING, but if owners Midge Jolly and Tom Weyant are working in one of their salt houses, stop in for a look. Call for an order form or look on their web site for locations in the Keys where you can buy their very distinctive products.

GREAT WHITE HERON NATIONAL WILDLIFE REFUGE
28950 Watson Boulevard, Big Pine Key: 305-872-2239
http://www.fws.gov/Refuges/profiles/index.cfm?id=41582
Established in 1938 as a haven for great white herons, migratory birds, and other wildlife, the refuge is located in the lower Florida Keys and consists of almost 200,000 acres of open water and islands that are north of the primary Keys from Marathon to Key West. The islands account for approximately 7,600 acres and are primarily mangroves with some of the larger islands containing pine rockland and tropical hardwood hammock habitats. This vast wilderness area, known locally as the "backcountry," provides critical nesting, feeding, and resting areas for more than 250 species of birds.
Great white herons are a white color-phase of great blue herons and are only found in the Florida Keys. The refuge was created to protect great white herons from extinction since the population was decimated by the demand for feathered hats. Protection of great white herons was successful, and these magnificent powder-white birds can be observed

feeding on tidal-flats around hundreds of backcountry islands each dawn and dusk.

NATIONAL KEY DEER REFUGE
28950 Watson Blvd., Big Pine Key: 305-872-2239
http://www.fws.gov/nationalkeydeer
9,200 acres of land that includes pine rockland forests, tropical hardwood hammocks, freshwater wetlands, salt marsh wetlands, and mangrove forests. Established to protect and preserve key deer, however, they also contain 17 listed species such as Lower Keys marsh rabbit, and silver rice rat.

BLUE HOLE
Key Deer Boulevard, Off U.S. 1, Mile Marker 30, Big Pine Key
http://www.florida-keys-guide.com/big-pine-key.html
To get there, turn right at Big Pine Key's only traffic light at Key Deer Boulevard (take the left fork immediately after the turn) and continue 1-1/2 miles to the observation-site parking lot, on your left. This is a former rock quarry now filled with fresh water, the walk to it is about ½ hour to an hour from the parking lot but the beauty makes it worth it. Word of caution: This place is home to alligators that are perfectly happy resting on the shoreline soaking up the sun. Don't bother them.

ATTRACTIONS KEY WEST

AUDUBON HOUSE & TROPICAL GARDENS
205 Whitehead St., Key West: 305-294-2116
http://www.audubonhouse.com WEBSITE DOWN AT PRESSTIME
ADMISSION: a modest fee.
A prime example of early Key West architecture, this 19th century home offers a respite from the hustle and bustle of downtown Key West. Included in the price of admission is a self-guided tour that will take you not only through the gardens, but through the house as well appreciating many of its gorgeous antiques, Audubon prints and historical photos. (They have about 30 of his first-edition illustrations.) Their gift shop is quite impressive.

COMPASS ROSE CHARTERS
1801 N. Roosevelt Blvd., Key West, 305-395-3474
www.fishnkw.com
Offshore fishing, reef fishing, wreck fishing, backcountry trips, you name it, Capt. Mike Weinhofer will tailor the trip to meet your needs.

CONCH TOUR TRAIN
303 Front St., Key West: 305-294-5161
http://www.conchtourtrain.com
Admission fee varies.
Conch Tour Train - a good way to get the lay of the (is)land. The Conch Tour Train has taken millions of visitors all over the island in their bright yellow "trains" since 1958. The well-narrated 90-minute tour, covering more than 100 unusual and historic sites, acquaints you with

the layout of the town. Trains leave every thirty minutes from 9 a.m. until 4:30 p.m.

CURRY MANSION INN & MUSEUM
511 Caroline St., Key West: 305-294-5349
http://www.currymansion.com
Admission fee varies.
The ornate Curry Mansion, a lovely all-white Victorian structure, is built on the site of the 1855 homestead of Florida's first millionaire, William Curry. The striking facade, with pillars and balconies, was added at the turn of the last century by Curry's son Milton. Inside are beautifully proportioned high-ceilinged rooms, antique furnishings. The mansion offers an excellent historic example of "elegant Key West." Tours are self-guided as you explore 15 antique-filled rooms.

CUSTOM HOUSE MUSEUM
281 Front St., Key West: 305-295-6616
www.kwahs.org/visit/custom-house
Admission fee varies.
HOURS: Open daily from 9:30 a.m. – 4:30 p.m., Closed Christmas
This four-story architectural marvel, originally home home to the island's customs office, postal service, and district courts, is a tremendous exemplar of Richardsonian Romanesque architecture. The building opened in 1891 and was the site of many significant historical events. Today visitors can visit the award-winning museum and headquarters of the Key West Art & Historical society. Museum has two floors of exhibitions.

ERNEST HEMINGWAY HOME AND MUSEUM
907 Whitehead St., Key West: 305-294-1136

http://www.hemingwayhome.com
Admission fee varies.
Limited parking.
Built in 1851, this is one of the island's first homes to be outfitted with indoor plumbing and built-in fireplace. The famed author owned this house from 1931 until his death in 1961 where he lived with some 40 cats, some of which whose descendants still roam the grounds. (I've actually been swimming in the pool here. We'd been drinking (way too much) down at the **Chart Room** in the old **Pier House** and on a dare walked down, broke into the yard and went swimming in the pool naked.) If you don't do anything else but drink and have sex on your visit, at least do this. You might want to pick up one of his books. (Start with **The Complete Short Stories of Ernest Hemingway,** available at any online book retailer where you can get a used paperback for a couple of dollars.)

FANTASY FEST
http://www.fantasyfest.com/
This is Key West's annual (middle of October) answer to Mardi Gras. Unless you're into the heavily gay "scene," stay away. Room rates are exorbitant. But it's a riot.

FLAGLER STATION & OVERSEAS RAILWAY HISTOREUM
901 Caroline St., Key West: 305-293-8716
http://www.flaglerstation.net
Flagler Station - "The Eighth Wonder of the World." In 1905 Henry Flagler, one of the wealthiest men in the world, announced his plan to build a railway from Miami to Key West. Some laughed, some scoffed, and most agreed that it could not be done. Eight years, three hurricanes, $30 million (pre-income tax) dollars, and hundreds of lives lost, Flagler proved them wrong. Visit the museum and experience the thrill of riding down the Florida Keys in 1929 aboard the "railway that went to the sea." Learn about the Key West Extension, and the tragic demise of Flagler's dream in the devastating Labor Day hurricane of 1935.

FLORIDA KEYS ECO-DISCOVERY CENTER
35 E. Quay Rd., Key West: 305-809-4750
http://www.floridakeys.noaa.gov/eco_discovery.html
ADMISSION: free to the public
Outstanding exhibits at the Florida Keys Eco Discovery Center, such as this one devoted to Hardwood Hammocks, interpret the eco system of Key West and the Florida Keys. A terrific educational facility with over 6,400 square feet of exhibits, including a 74-seat movie theater. Highlights of the Center include an interactive map of the Keys, a replica of the Aquarius underwater laboratory, and an underwater video

camera that allows guests to observe coral spawning, assess damage from a boat grounding or monitor the health of a coral reef. The Center also features a high-definition film by renowned cinematographer Bob Talbot, computer interactive exhibits, murals, graphic displays with text and images, a live weather station and replicas of South Florida habitats such as mangroves, complete with sounds. Mote Marine Laboratory's Baby Conch Farm has moved to the Eco-Discovery Center and is now part of its Living Reef exhibit. They have free on-site parking. This is a fun thing to do in Key West for the whole family.

FORT EAST MARTELLO
3501 S. Roosevelt Blvd., Key West: 305-296-3913
www.kwahs.org/visit/fort-east-martello
Admission fee varies.
HOURS: Open daily from 9:30 a.m. – 4:30 p.m., Closed Christmas
Construction began in1862 on this Fort by the U.S. Army but it was never finished. In 1950, the Key West Art & Historical Society opened it as its first museum. Explore the preserved battlement's collection of relics from the Civil War, learn about the wrecking and cigar-manufacturing industries which shaped the Florida Keys, and view the art exhibitions of folk artist Mario Sanchez and sculptor Stanley Papio.

FORT JEFFERSON TOURS
Key West Ferry Terminal, 100 Grinnell Street, in the Historic Seaport,
800-634-0939
http://www.drytortugas.com/fort-jefferson

If you possibly have the time while in Key West, you've got to make the trip to Fort Jefferson out in the Dry Tortugas (*tortuga* means turtle in Spanish). The little islands—barely sandbars—were named by the Spanish when they saw a huge number of turtles that lived here. This is a very interesting place for being a fort stuck in the middle of nowhere. It was built before (and during) the Civil War, and was turned into a prison during the war. (Inmates called the place "Devil's Island" because it was a pestilential hellhole where people got malaria and died by the dozen.) The fort is located on Garden Key, which covers about 10 acres.

The most famous inmate was Dr. Samuel Mudd (ancestor of the CBS newsman Roger Mudd), who was convicted of helping John Wilkes Booth after he assassinated Lincoln, though in truth Mudd had no knowledge of the plot. (He was later released.) John Ford made a (pro-Confederate) film in 1936 about Dr. Mudd called *The Prisoner of Shark Island* starring Warner Baxter and Gloria Stuart (who played Old Rose in *Titanic*). I've seen it. It's good. You can get it on Netflix. Over the cell where Mudd lived you'll see a quote from Dante's *Inferno*: "Whoever So Entereth Here Leaveth All Hopes Behind." Not the cheeriest thought. The isolation and loneliness drove many prisoners mad. Besides the ever-present malaria, there were other maladies to confront: cholera, dysentery, sunstroke. Harrison Herrick of the 110th New York Regiment wrote in his diary (you can see it here): "One of the guards, of the Delaware Artillery, shot himself through the head. He was crazy. Weather fair and pleasant."

Mudd was released by special pardon of President Andrew Johnson in 1867 after helping to quell a yellow fever epidemic, taking over when the fort's doctor succumbed.

It's also interesting to note that Cubans who land here are instantly permitted to come into the U.S. Some arrive every month to take advantage of that little twist in our foreign policy.

It was called (and it still is) "the largest brick structure in the Western Hemisphere," and it's the oddest thing to see this huge mound of bricks rise out of the sea as you approach by sea. The place is really quite splendid. When you cross the old moat, they'll tell you it was once filled with sharks to dissuade the prisoners from escaping. (It worked!)

After taking the tour you get free with the price of your voyage, go to the little museum and buy the book, *America's Fortress* and take your own tour.

YANKEE FREEDOM II DAY TRIPS
Passage fees vary.
800-634-0939.
www.yankeefreedom.com

You can take a day trip out (leave Key West at 8 a.m., return a bit after 5) on this high-speed ocean-going catamaran specifically designed for carrying passengers safely across the 70 miles of open water from Key West to the Dry Tortugas National Park where Fort Jefferson is situated. Ship is 100' long and 60' wide, a broad and stable vessel certified to carry 250 passengers; however, to maximize the comfort of each guest, they limit each trip to 150 passengers. The 7 remote islands you will visit are called the Dry Tortugas. En route, they have an onboard naturalist who will give you an orientation about the area and the national park's surroundings. During your voyage, you will enjoy the beautiful scenery of the Marquesa Islands, Boca Grande, have an opportunity to see turtles and dolphins, and listen to pirate legends. You can travel inside the main cabin in air-conditioned comfort or outside on one of the observation decks. Three restrooms, fresh water rinse shower, full galley serving snacks, soft drinks, beer, wine, mixed drinks (on return trip only), film, and souvenirs. **Price includes admission to the Fort, a guided tour, free snorkeling equipment and a good-sized breakfast and lunch served aboard the boat.**

The trip out runs 2 ½ hours each way, which gives you about 4 to 4 ½ hours to explore the Fort on the day trip.

Two excursions: day trips and overnight camping. They've been ferrying folks to Fort Jefferson since 1977.

SEAPLANE TOURS
www.drytortugas.com
Fees vary.
I much prefer the seaplane trip out to the ferry because I'm usually in a big hurry. If you've got time to kill, the ferry is the more leisurely way to go. The best thing about taking a seaplane out to Fort Jefferson is that you have the place pretty much to yourself until the ferries show up with a couple of hundred people. Then the place is overrun. It's pricey, but it's worth it.

FORT ZACHARY TAYLOR STATE PARK
Southard St on Truman Annex, Key West, 305-292-6713
www.floridastateparks.org/park/Fort-Taylor
This is the southernmost Florida state park, located at the end of Southard Street in the Truman Annex. The fort was one of a series built in the mid-1800s to defend the southeastern coastline. Completed in 1866, Fort Zachary Taylor played important roles in the Civil War and Spanish-American War. Guided tours of the fort are available daily. Key West's favorite beach, located at the southern end of the park, provides opportunities for picnicking, swimming, snorkeling, and fishing. Visitors can also enjoy a short nature trail and bicycling within the park. (In case you didn't know, Taylor was the 12th U.S. president, dying after only 16 months in office of a stomach ailment. He rose to prominence as "Old Rough & Ready," the general who vanquished the enemy in the Mexican-American War.

GHOSTS & GRAVESTONES NIGHT TOUR
501 Front St., Key West: 866-955-0668
www.ghostsandgravestones.com
Admission fee varies.
HOURS: 7 p.m. – 10 p.m. – seven days a week.
Step aboard the Trolley of the Doomed and experience the dark, scary side of Key West. It's a nighttime trip with a Ghost Host who guides you through the streets of historic Old Town where you visit sites like the Grotto of our Lady of Lourdes, the African Slave Cemetery, and St. Paul's Church. Ghost tours run rain or shine. Wear comfortable walking shoes.

HARRY TRUMAN'S LITTLE WHITE HOUSE
111 Front St., Key West: 305-294-9911
http://www.trumanlittlewhitehouse.com
Admission fee varies.
The restored winter White House was used by Presidents Truman, Eisenhower & Kennedy. Harry Truman found this tropical island the perfect winter getaway. He chose this West Indian style dwelling to be his working winter "White House" for his vacations from 1946-1952. Truman loved being outdoors in Key West. In the morning he would often go to the beach. Also, he was an avid fisherman and whenever he could he loved to fish the Key West waters. Situated on the former Navy property known as Truman Annex, with entrance through the Presidential Gates on Whitehead St., it has been restored with total authenticity. Guided tours daily. Also offers a free self-guided botanical tour.

KEY WEST AQUARIUM
1 Whitehead St., Key West: 888-544-5927
http://www.keywestaquarium.com
Admission fee varies.

Key West Aquarium guide showing a live nurse shark to visitors. When the Key West Aquarium opened for business during the Great Depression in 1934 it was the island's first tourist attraction. At the time, Key West was the only city completely on federal relief after turning over its charter to state and federal governments. The Aquarium, constructed 1932-1934, was a major part of Key West's attempt at economic recovery by advertising their city as "America's Caribbean Island." Today, the Aquarium educates, fascinates, and amuses visitors to Key West with unique and wonderful marine creatures. Shark feeding, Touch Tank, and stingray exhibits are not to be missed.

KEY WEST ART & HISTORICAL SOCIETY
281 Front St., Key West: 305-295-6616
www.kwahs.org
Key West Art & Historical Society has a mission to preserve, interpret and exhibit culturally-significant art, architecture and artifacts of the Florida Keys. The Society oversees three national landmarks: Custom House Museum, Lighthouse & Keeper's Quarters, and Fort East Mortello.

KEY WEST BUTTERFLY & NATURE CONSERVATORY
1316 Duval St., Key West: 305-296-2988
http://www.keywestbutterfly.com
Admission fee varies.
You will have a unique opportunity to observe butterflies and birds in a tropical setting. The Butterfly & Nature Conservatory is one of Key West's newer attractions and really in a category of its own. A large, glass atrium has been filled with lush tropical vegetation, colorful and exotic butterflies, and tropical birds. Flowering plants line the winding pathways as some 50 different types of butterflies enjoy the habitat.

Don't be surprised if one lands on your colorful shirt. They will even sip nectar from your hand. All the while enjoy the serenity and beauty of the climate controlled (for the creatures, not you) environment. Great gift shop with many unique items.

KEY WEST CEMETERY
701 Passover Ln., Key West, 305-292-8177
www.friendsofthekeywestcemetery.com/
Eccentricity at its best, this quirky cemetery is full of funny stories and ghostly hauntings. Many tombs are stacked high because of soil conditions. If you plan on walking through the cemetery, we suggest you pick up a guide specific to the cemetery as many of its must-sees are difficult to find.

KEY WEST FIREHOUSE MUSEUM
1024 Grinnell, Key West: 305-849-0678
www.keywestfirehousemuseum.com
ADMISSION: Free, donations appreciated
HOURS: By appointment only, call Alex at 305-797-8417 or Rich at 305-923-8917
Built in 1907, Fire Station No. 3, located at the corner of Grinnell and Virginia Streets, is one of the oldest fire stations in the state of Florida.

KEY WEST GHOST TOUR
432 Greene St., Key West: 305-395-1435
http://www.hauntedtours.com
Admission fee varies.

This will take you on a lantern-led evening stroll down Old Town's shadowy lanes, listening to the tales of ghosts, ghouls and legends that haunt the island. Reservations are strongly recommended.

KEY WEST GHOST & MYSTERIES TOURS
429 Caroline St., Key West: 305-292-2040
www.keywestghostandmysteriestour.com
Admission fee varies.
HOURS: Tours Depart Nightly at 9 p.m.
This 90-minute stroll takes you a tour of the haunted and hidden side of the Island that most visitors never get to see. The guides are master storytellers and bring these ghost stories to life. Tour highlights include: Haunted Victorian Mansions, Key West's Oldest Graveyard, Enchanted Robert the Doll, Haunted Pubs, Count Von Cosel and Eleyna, Original Hanging Tree, and The Watcher. Take your camera.

KEY WEST LIGHTHOUSE MUSEUM
938 Whitehead St., Key West: 305-294-0012
http://www.kwahs.com
ADMISSION: fee varies.
If you can muster the energy to climb 88 confining steps, then you will be rewarded with breathtaking panoramic views of Key West and the ocean. Opened in 1848, its story is displayed in a small museum that used to be the keeper's quarters.

KEY WEST'S SHIPWRECK HISTOREUM
1 Whitehead St., Key West: 305-292-8990
www.keywestshipwreck.com
Admission fee varies.
This museum is the place to indulge your romantic shipwreck fantasies. You can see movies, artifacts and even meet a real life wrecker who

will be more than happy to talk to you about the wrecking industry that plagued early Key West.

KEY WEST TROPICAL FOREST & BOTANICAL GARDEN
5210 College Rd., Key West: 305-296-1504
www.kwbgs.org
Admission fee varies.
HOURS: Open Daily, 10 a.m. to 4 p.m.
Closed Thanksgiving, Christmas, New Years day and July 4
This is the only "frost-free" botanical garden in the continental United States. The Garden is home to many endangered and threatened flora and fauna and advocates the importance of native plants and species through education in a natural conservation habitat. The Forest has two of the last remaining fresh water ponds in the Keys and is a major stopping point for neo-tropical birds. The Forest and Garden is filled with butterflies, birds, plants, beautiful flowers and a hidden pond. Center offers a short film and photo exhibition. 8 self-guided information tours, two wetland habitats and two butterfly gardens.

MALLORY SQUARE
400 Wall St., Key West, 305-809-3700
www.mallorysquare.com
Sunsets in Key West (the ones I remember, anyway) have always included this weird sort of circuslike ritual on Mallory Square. I have no idea when it actually started. But it was going strong when I made my first visit in the 1960s. It happens every day, rain or shine. All the burned-out hippies and rummies turn out. There are jugglers, sword

swallowers, unicyclists, guitar players, food vendors and other assorted oddball characters. You don't have to see this every evening, but you have to do it once. And—don't forget—the sunset in the Gulf is what started this to begin with. So make sure you take your eyes off the freaks long enough to enjoy it. You won't see a sunset like this at home every night. No, sir!

MEL FISHER MARITIME HERITAGE MUSEUM
200 Greene St., Key West: 305-294-2633
http://www.melfisher.org
Admission fee varies.
Incredible sunken treasures are revealed at the Mel Fisher Maritime Museum.
World famous treasure hunter Mel Fisher uncovered the wreck of the Spanish galleon Atocha in 1985, after an exhausting search which took over 18 years and cost him the life of his son, a professional diver. The world of shipwreck archaeology is the theme of this awesome museum where you will see the ropes of pure gold and fist-sized emeralds that were recovered. Lift a real gold bar and view a number of artifacts. They continue to look for more treasure, and repeat Mel's famous saying "Today's the day." You'll never look at the ocean the same way.

OLD TOWN TROLLEY TOURS
1 Whitehead St, Key West, 305-296-6688
http://www.trolleytours.com/key-west
Admission fee varies.
The Trolley, as it is locally known, makes 10 stops on its route throughout the historic area of Key West. The Old Town Trolley differs from the Conch Tour Train only in giving you the opportunity to disembark at 11 different locations to be able to take in the attractions in that neighborhood – and then to reboard and continue the tour. This is the way to go if you have the time to explore the parts of Key West you are interested in. Plus, your paid fare is good for the full day - allowing you to ride as many times as you like during the normal business hours for that day. Along the way, expect a very good narration of local history, tropical life, and the quirks of Key West.

RED BARN THEATRE
319 Duval St., Key West: 305-296-9911
redbarntheatre.com/
Considered on the best professional theatres in Florida, the Red Barn has a year round schedule of current hit plays starring professional actors. When they are between shows, the theatre is used for musicals, cabarets and concerts. Well worth checking out their site to see what's happening when you're in town.

RIPLEY'S BELIEVE IT OR NOT
108 Duval St., Key West: 305-293-9939
www.ripleys.com/keywest
Admission fee varies.
HOURS: Open 365 days a year from 9am to 11pm
Here you have the Key West version of Ripley's Believe it or Not! With an Odditorium over 8,000 square feet featuring over 500 bizarre and unusual exhibits. These artifacts collected by Robert Ripley are unique and extraordinary and include a genuine shrunken torso, see an extremely rare white buffalo, a beautiful carving of a landscape made entirely out of camel bone, and a car that has been covered in over 10,000 dimes.

SHIPWRECK TREASURES MUSEUM
1 Whitehead St., Key West: 305-292-8990
http://www.keywestshipwreck.com
The Shipwreck Treasures Museum is home to the last Key West's Lookout Towers. At one point in its history, Key West was the richest city in the United States. Wrecking, or the salvaging of ships run aground on the reef, was big business in the 19th century. Meet the men who risked their lives and fortunes as you enter the unique world of an 1856 wrecker's warehouse. You'll meet the master wrecker and his crew in a warehouse filled with booty and bounty of the reefs and cargo from the past. Then climb the lookout towers, originally used by salvors to observe wrecks on the reef, and enjoy a view of the historic district and the waters that surround Key West. This is a museum that the whole family can enjoy.

THE SOUTHERNMOST HOUSE & MUSEUM
1400 Duval St., Key West: 305-296-3141
http://www.southernmosthouse.com
At the end of upper Duval Street is Key West's Southernmost House. One of the most striking buildings in all of Key West is the Southernmost House & Museum. The structure is an impressive example of Queen Anne Victorian architecture and sits proudly overlooking the Atlantic Ocean. The museum boasts a collection of important and interesting documents, many of which are signed by presidents of the United States, including John F. Kennedy's inaugural address. Visitors are welcome (for a few dollars more) to spend the day poolside, enjoying the cocktails and impressive property.

TROPIC CINEMA
416 Eaton St., Key West: 305-396-4944
tropiccinema.com/
You'll wish you had this old Art Deco cinema in the town where you live: it's impeccably maintained, has a bar inside, serves popcorn that smells like the popcorn you remember as a child, serves *real butter*. Oh, and yeah, it shows movies. Not just current Hollywood fare, but also interesting indie films. Great place to hang out on a rainy say.

THE WRECKER'S MUSEUM
THE OLDEST HOUSE IN KEY WEST
1 Whitehead St, Key West: 305-292-8900
www.keywestshipwreck.com
Key West's oldest house, the Wreckers House, on Duval Street. This conch cottage is known as the oldest house on the island, having been built in 1829. It was the home to a famous wrecker, Captain Francis B. Watlington. (Don't you love that name?) The property has three

buildings, the main house, the kitchen house, and the exhibit pavilion, which face a garden with benches. On display, along with the maritime artifacts are works of art by Mario Sanchez, Key West's famous folk art wood carver.

KEY WEST CHARTERS – TOURS

Note that several excursions, such as seaplane trips to **Fort Jefferson**, are listed in the **Attractions** chapter.

ADIRONDACK III/CLASSIC HARBOR LINE
202 Williams St., Key West: 305-293-7245
www.sail-keywest.com
Fees vary.
HOURS: Open seven days a week.
Take an exciting cruise on the most elegant vessel in the local schooner fleet, the Adirondack III   Choose from a variety of options: Mimosa Morning Sails, Day Sails, Champagne Sunset Sails, Full Moon, and Star-Gazer Sails. Private Charters available.

ANDY GRIFFITHS FISHING CHARTERS
6810 Front St, Stock Island, 305-296-2639
www.fishandy.com
RATES: Customized rates
HOURS: 3 hours to 3 days
Captain Andy takes his boats on a variety of fishing charters, from Tortugas fishing trips out of Key West, Florida to overnight fishing to Fort Jefferson, Dry Tortugas and Marquesas Keys. Serious fishing trips and deep sea fishing.

BAREFOOT BILLY'S JET SKI TOURS
701 Seminole St., Key West: 305-900-3088
www.barefootbillys.com
RATES: Rates vary depending on date, time, and length of tour.
HOURS: 9 a.m. –6 p.m.
For the past 20 years, Barefoot Billy's has been providing visitors with some of the island's most exciting adventures including guided jetski tours. Take a ride on a Yamaha Waverunners and cruise around the island on a 28-mile, 2-hour guided jet ski tour. You'll see an array of Florida Key' wildlife as you speed through the Caribbean Waters from the Atlantic Ocean to the Gulf of Mexico and then back.

BLUE EYED TRADER
5555 College Rd, Key West: 305-393-1799
www.fishingwithron.com
Captain Ron DeLuc is your host on this fine charter boat operation. He's been fishing these waters (and all up and down the Keys) since 1980. Wife Nina is often onboard to assist. Fine and friendly people.

CLASSIC HARBOR LINE
202 Williams St., Key West: 305-293-7245
www.sail-keywest.com
Sunset sailing trips have long been popular in Key West. You can't go wrong by choosing to go with these guys. Their ship the *America 2.0* is the best. (They also have another ship, the historic *Adirondack III.*) You get a 2-hour sailing cruise aboard this 105-foot yacht that boasts 3,600 square feet of canvas, teak decks, brass and mahogany woodwork. Free beer, champagne, soft drinks as you watch the sun go down. (While food is not included, if you want to picnic, you can pick up a box lunch at the **Schooner Wharf Bar** right near the embarkation point. Weddings, corporate trips, private charters.

CLEARLY UNIQUE CHARTERS GLASS-BOTTOM KAYAKS
231 Margaret St., West, 305-747-8651
www.clearlyuniquecharters.com
Admission fee varies.
HOURS: 10 a.m. – 1 p.m., 2 p.m. – 5 p.m.
Kayak the backcountry of Key West and see all the waters including underwater as these tours combine kayaking and snorkeling aboard your glass bottom kayak. Each kayak fits two. You'll see the mangrove islands above the water and the eco-system of the ocean floor below. Excursion begins aboard a 33-foot Beach Cat catamaran.

DANCING DOLPHIN SPIRITS CHARTERS
5710 US #1, MM5, Key West, 305-304-7562
www.captainvictoria.com
Admission fee varies.
HOURS: Departing: 8 -12, 12:15-4:15, 8 - 3
Travel the waterways of the Key West area with Captain Victoria. You'll skim across the waves listening to classical music. You'll see cormorants popping up from below the surface or flapping dramatically into flight, ibis, herons, frigate birds and osprey flying and fishing or sunbathing.

DANGER CHARTERS – WESTIN MARINA
Westin Hotel Marina, corner of Whitehead St. & Greene St.: 305-304-7999
www.dangercharters.com
RATES: vary
Sail to another world and time, a place where wildlife is still "wild." You'll feel like you stepped back in time traveling the Florida Keys backcountry on a traditional, shallow-draft sailing craft.

EASY DAY CHARTERS
711 Palm Avenue, Garrison Bight Marina, Key West: 305-797-7005
www.easydaycharters.com
Most charter operations in the Keys will tailor the tour to fit your specifications, and no one does it better than the folks here at Easy Day. Fishing excursions, snorkeling, scuba, dolphin, romantic, eco-tours, visit the sandbars and beaches, whatever you want.

FURY WATER ADVENTURES
241 Front St, Key West: 888-976-0899
www.furycat.com
RATES: Rates vary per adventure.
Take an excursion on the crystal blue waters surrounding the Keys' island paradise. Choose from a variety of adventures: Reef Snorkeling or Sunset Cruises/Sails aboard the Fury Catamaran, thrills in the air with Fury Parasailing, or Reef Eco-Tours aboard the Fury Glass Bottom Boat. Private Charters are also available. Fury's Combo Packages and Fury's Ultimate Adventure are available which include Reef Snorkeling, Parasailing, Jet Skiing, Kayaking, Rock Climbing, Water Trampoline and more.

KEY WEST BIPLANE TOURS
Key West International Airport, 3469 S. Roosevelt Blvd: 305-851-8359
www.keywestbiplanes.com
Rates vary. Open cockpit flight 7 days a week from 10 a.m. – sunset in a pristine 1942 WACO UPF-7 equipped with dual cameras that will record for posterity your plane ride on DVD.

KEY WEST ECO TOURS
201 William St., Key West: 305-294-7245
www.keywestecotours.com
All in One Eco Tour
Admission fee varies.
HOURS: 9 a.m. to 1:30 p.m., 2 p.m. to 6:30 p.m.
Key West Eco Tours offers a variety of adventures: sail on board a 31' Catamaran designed for shallow water (18" draft) or kayak around mangrove islands and snorkel a marine nursery teeming with tropical fish. You can also take a 4.5 hour Sail, Kayak, Snorkel tour. Tours start at the Key West National Wildlife Refuge west of Key West. Enjoy a kayak tour around the mangrove islands looking for small sharks, sting rays, fish, and a variety of birds or snorkel on a soft coral and sponge garden, looking for lobsters, nurse sharks, conchs, eels, and variety of other marine life. Included is a light lunch, water & soft drinks, towels, and all your equipment.

KEY WEST SEAPLANES
3471 South Roosevelt Blvd., Key West: 305-293-9300
www.keywestseaplanecharters.com
RATES: Call for rates.
Explore Florida, the Bahamas and the Caribbean in an amphibious seaplane that has the ability to land on water or land. Key West Seaplanes also offers private service to the exclusive Little Palm Island.

HYDRO THUNDER WATERSPORTS HYATT
601 Front St., Key West: 305-294-7000
www.hydrothunderofkeywest.com
RATES: Call for pricing, reservations, or any other questions:
Jet Skis, Tours and Boats: 305-295-7525   Motor Scooters and Electric Cars: 305-294-7000

HOURS: 7 days a week from 9 a.m. to sunset.
Enjoy the thrill of a wet and wild ride on Key West waters on a Yamaha 4-stroke Waverunner. Rent on your own for half or hour rides but the best is the 27 mile professionally guided Jet Ski Tour circling Key West and nearby islands. You can speed up to 50 mph over crystal clear waters where you can see all types of tropical sea life. The tour makes stops for photo ops. On land you can rent a Yamaha or Honda motor scooter to travel around Key West.

ISLAND SAFARI JET SKI TOURS
5016 5th Ave., Key West: 305-879-2124
www.islandsafaritourskeywest.com
Admission fee varies.
HOURS: Every day 9 a.m. – 6 p.m.
Local tour guides, who know the waters like pirates of the seas, take you on an adventurous 27 mile tour where you enjoy Key West's coastal views, wild life, mangrove islands, the Southernmost point of the US 90 miles to Cuba, jumping dolphins, sea turtles, beautiful, sandy beaches and coral reefs and of course the spectacular turquoise Caribbean sea. Bring a water-proof camera.

LAZY DOG KAYAK & PADDLEBOARD TOURS
5114 Overseas Hwy., Key West: 305-295-9898
www.lazydog.com
RATES: vary
HOURS: Call for reservations.
Walk on the water and view the sea life with a standup paddleboard, a combination of surfing and kayaking. Fun for the entire family. on your experience. Great for beginners and experienced paddlers. Kayak rentals and tours available. On-site shop with t-shirts, caps, accessories and paddleboards.

SEBAGO WATERSPORTS
205 Elizabeth St., Key West: 800-507-9955
www.keywestsebago.com
RATES: Rates vary depending on adventure.
HOURS: 10 a.m. – 5 p.m. (Most trips return at 4 p.m.)
Key West Sebago offers packages for sunset cruises, dolphin charters, snorkeling adventures, weddings, kayaking, and parasailing. Catamaran snorkeling travel adventures includes sailing on the only live coral reef in the U.S.

SUNSET WATERSPORTS
201 William St., Key West: 855-378-6386
www.sunsetwatersportskeywest.com
RATES: Rates vary per adventure.
HOURS: Call for reservations.
Sunset Watersports offers an exciting list of water adventures including: reef snorkel, parasailing, waverunners, sunset cruise, safari snorkel tour, and the all-day water adventure on the 65 foot luxury catamaran and enjoy 11 watersports activities.

VENUS CHARTERS
Garrison Bight Marina: 305-304-1181
www.venuscharters.com
RATES: Charters fees vary
HOURS: Call for reservations.
Venus Charters is the only Lesbian owned and operated charter boat in South Florida.
Charters available for tackle fishing, exploring wild dolphins or an uninhabited island.

WILD ABOUT DOLPHINS
6000 Peninsula Ave., Stock Island, Key West: 305-294-5026
www.wildaboutdolphins.com
Captain Sheri Sullenger knows more about dolphins than you probably need to know, but if you really want to get close to the dolphins and learn about them in more than a cursory manner, this is the tour for you. But Captain Sheri can also take you on swimming and snorkeling trips, picnics, tailor the excursion to fit your needs aboard her boat, the *Amazing Grace*. Also, you get a private day member pass to the **Key West Harbour Yacht Club** if you book with her, giving you access to their bars, restaurant, pool, sauna and fitness center. Free parking and a ships' store.

Chapter 6

SHOPPING & SERVICES

UPPER & MIDDLE KEYS

ISLAND SMOKE SHOP
103400 Overseas Hwy. at MM 103.4, Key Largo: 305-453-4014
http://www.islandsmokeshop.com
Premium cigars at a great price for every budget. They will be happy to sell you singles, bundles or boxes of your favorite cigar brands. Large walk-in humidor, they offer 1200 different brands of cigars.

KMART
5561 Overseas Hwy., Marathon: 305-743-9434
www.kmart.com
It's typical in the sense that it's a Kmart store but a little smaller than most. Has a little souvenir section. I never thought I'd be listing a Kmart in one of my books, but here it is.

RAIN BARREL VILLAGE OF ARTISTS AND CRAFTSPEOPLE
86700 Overseas Hwy. at MM 86.7, Islamorada: 305-852-3084

www.keysdirectory.com/rainbarrel/
This little village is home to the studios and galleries of many artists. In this maze of curious little shops you will find pottery, jewelry and stained glass being designed right in front of you. Set amidst quaint tropical gardens, you will also find a vegetarian café.

SANDAL FACTORY
5195 Overseas Hwy., Marathon: 305-743-5778
http://www.sandalfactory.com
This is the place to stop if you need a t-shirt, flip-flops, bathing suit, board shorts or anything of the like. Prices run the gamut from cheap to expensive and they'll have you out in no time at all.

SHELL WORLD
U.S. 1 at MM 97.5 Bayside (follow signs), Key Largo: 305-852-8245
http://www.shellworldflkeys.com
Seashells galore. From Florida and around the world, here you will finds shells in all sizes, shapes and colors. You'll be amazed.

SHOPPING LOWER KEYS

ARTISTS IN PARADISE GALLERY
221 Key Deer Blvd., Big Pine Key: 305-872-1828
http://www.artistsinparadise.com/
Established in 1994, this art gallery exhibits quite a number of artists and their work. Both the mediums and the artwork are constantly changing.

BIG PINE BICYCLE CENTER
31 County Rd., Big Pine Key: 305-872-0130
http://www.bigpinebikes.com/
The place for everything bicycle. Rentals, repairs, parts and accessories. New bicycle sales, KHS bikes, free agent BMX bikes. Knowledgeable staff.

BIG PINE TRUE VALUE BUILDERS SUPPLY
30770 Overseas Hwy., Big Pine Key: 305-872-2337
http://ww3.truevalue.com/bigpinetruevalue
Hardware store and building supply store.

CASA MAR FRESH SEAFOOD MARKET
90775 Old Hwy, Tavernier, 305-440-3935
www.casamarseafoodmarket.com
If you're looking for fresh seafood, this is the place. Here you'll find fresh fillets, Ambejack, Flounder, Grouper, Snapper, Mahi Mahi, Salmon, Swordfish, Salmon, and Tuna. The market also offers oysters, Stone Crab Claws, Softshell Crab, King Crab Legs, and the list goes on. Check out their online market for a complete list.

OUT OF THE BLUE GALLERY & GIFTS
29842 Overseas Hwy., Big Pine Key: 305-872-8864
Great little gift shop where you will find jewelry by local artisans, delightful books and many other interesting curiosities.

SHOPPING KEY WEST

The main area for shopping in Key West is the street where everything else happens: Duval Street. Here you will find such national chain retailers like Banana Republic and the Gap alongside independent clothing boutiques, t-shirt and sandal shops, kitschy gift shops, local street vendors, jewelry stores and some larger stores.

In an effort to keep this interesting, below you will find a list of stores that you might find more curious than your typical t-shirt and bikini store. Enjoy!

CLINTON SQUARE MARKET
291 Front St., Key West: 305-296-6825
An over air-conditioned mall of kiosks and stalls designed for the many cruise-ship passengers who never venture beyond this super-commercial zone. There are some coffee and candy shops, and some high-priced hats and shoes. There's also a free (and clean) restroom.

COCKTAILS! KEY WEST
808 Duval St., Key West: 305-292-1190
A shop that celebrates the art of drink with coasters, glasses, bottle openers, ice buckets, shot glasses, and martini sets. Everything to stock a bar.

DIVERS DIRECT OUTLET
535 Greene St., Key West: 305-293-5122
www.diversdirect.com
The place for all things scuba. Diving regulators, masks, buoyancy compensator, air tank fills, scuba gear and beachwear.

FAIRVILLA MEGASTORE
Email: debra@fairvilla.com
524 Front St., Key West: 305-292-0448
www.fairvilla.com
Thousands of sexy Halloween costumes here in the store or online. Starline, Coquette, Leg Avenue, Baci and Dreamgirl.

FAST BUCK'S AT HOME
726 Caroline St., Key West: 305-294-1304.
www.fastbucksathome.com
For 37 years in their Duval Street location, Fast Buck Freddie's offered everything from bed linens to candlesticks, clothing, whatever. They're still open, but in this new location, 10-5 daily.

FAUSTO'S FOOD PALACE
522 Fleming St., Key West: 305-296-5663
www.faustos.com
Local grocery store that specializes in gourmet, organic and specialty foods.

THE GREEN PINEAPPLE
1130 Duval St., Key West, 305-509-7378
www.greenpineapplekeywest.com
An eclectic shop with an interesting collection of gifts, fair trade, hand-crafted, organic, recycle and vintage. You'll find "green" products, body scents, scrubs and creams, jewelry, kitchenware, and clothing.

ISLAND LOVE STORY
804 Caroline St., Key West: 305-293-8555
www.islandlovestory.com
A beautiful home décor shop filled with home furnishings and accessories including furniture, lamps, mirrors, sisal rugs, custom floor mats and unique garden items.

KERMIT'S KEY WEST KEY LIME SHOPPE
200 Elizabeth St., Key West: 800-376-0806
www.keylimeshop.com
A shop that celebrates all that's key lime including: Key Lime Cookies, Key Lime Salsa, Key Lime Chutney, Key Lime Taffy, Key Lime Jelly Beans, Key Lime Tea, Key Lime Olive Oil and of course there's plenty of Key Lime pie.

KEY WEST ISLAND BOOKSTORE
513 Fleming St., Key West: 305-294-2904
http://keywestislandbooks.com

New, used, and rare books, and specializes in fiction by residents of the Keys, including Ernest Hemingway, Tennessee Williams, Shel Silverstein, Ann Beattie, Richard Wilbur, and John Hersey.

KEY WEST KEY LIME PIE CO.
511 Greene St., Key West: 305-517-6720
http://www.keywestkeylimepieco.com
Offers a variety of key lime products, from their award-winning handmade pies to their slices of key lime pie dipped in rich chocolate and served on a stick. Check out their Key Lime Pie Bar. They offer key lime jellies both regular and hot with a hint of pepper, key lime chipotle BBQ sauces, marinades and a host of other zesty Key Lime favorites. No longer just a shop for key lime products, try their delicious blueberry, blood orange, and mango pies.

KEY WEST WINERY
103 Simonton St., Key West: 305-916-5343
http://www.thekeywestwinery.com
Their wines are non-traditional because they do not use any grapes to produce them. Instead, the winemaker has produced a line of wines that use fruits, berries and citrus. The result has been an assortment of wines that are full-bodied, flavorful, and with surprising bouquets.

KEYS FRAMING & ART SUPPLIES
1103 Truman Ave., Key West: 240-7775
www.facebook.com/keysframing
Art shop for the seasoned artist or novice. Will frame your art and make old photos look like new. Exhibits art.

KILWIN'S CHOCOLATES
505 Duval St., Key West: 305-320-0986
www.kilwins.com/keywest
Kilwins Chocolate, Fudge, and Ice Cream shop offers friendly service and serves the world's best Mackinac Island fudge, Original Recipe ice cream and fresh candy and chocolate treats made in the store.

KWEST LIQUORS
705 Duval St., Key West: 305-294-5995
www.kwestliquorstore.com
One-stop shopping for beers, wines, cigars, cigarettes, lottery tickets, snacks, ice cream, and sundries. Serving breakfast & lunch.

MEL FISHER'S TREASURES
200 Greene St., Key West: 800-434-1399
www.melfisher.com
Treasures (and reproductions) from the sunken *Atocha*: fleet rings, coins, emeralds, rings, silver bars, authentic coins, chains, collectors' treasures, Fisher Collection items, gold bars and discs, original art, replica Atocha coins, shipwreck replica jewelry, souvenirs, treasure books, treasure video.

NAILTINI NAIL BAY & DAY SPA
817 Duval St., Key West: 305-294-4443; www.nailtinikeywest.com
Whoever heard of a mani pedi place that serves you martinis while you have your extremities prettified? Well, this is Key West, don't forget. They'll offer you a martini, a mimosa, white wine. Professional service: facials, waxing, massage, spa quality manicure and pedicures.

PEPPERS OF KEY WEST
602 Greene St., Key West: 305-295-9333
http://www.peppersofkeywest.com
A hot-sauce-lover's heaven, with hundreds of variations, from mild to brutally spicy. Grab a seat at the tasting bar and be prepared to let your taste buds sizzle. TIP: Bring beer, and they'll let you taste some of their secret sauces.

GYMS

OLD TOWN FITNESS
1010 Truman Ave., Key West: 305-292-3999
www.oldtownfitness.com
Daily rates available for travelers. Large old school gym, mostly free weights, with more than 3,500 square feet of workout space. Personal trainers and indoor cycling classes.

PARADISE PILATES
328 William St., Key West: : 305-304-1726
www.paradisepilates.com
Group and private Pilates classes offered.

PILATES STUDIO OF KEY WEST
1901 Fogerty Ave., Key West: 305-517-6930
www.pilateskeywest.com
Enjoy the many spiritual, physical and health benefits of Pilates. Private, duo, and trio classes available. Pre-registration necessary.

INDEX

A

A&B LOBSTER HOUSE, 41
ADIRONDACK III/CLASSIC HARBOR LINE, 89
AFRICAN QUEEN, 64
ALABAMA JACK, 33
ALEXANDER'S GUESTHOUSE, 31
ALONZO & BERLIN'S LOBSTER HOUSE, 41
AMARA CAY RESORT, 10
AMBROSIA, 42
AMBROSIA KEY WEST, 17
ANDY GRIFFITHS FISHING CHARTERS, 89
ANGELINA GUEST HOUSE, 17
ANTONIA'S, 42
AQUA, 58
ARTISTS IN PARADISE GALLERY, 98
AUDUBON HOUSE & TROPICAL GARDENS, 74
AZUR, 42

B

B.O.'S FISH WAGON, 44
BACKCOUNTRY COWBOY OUTFITTERS, 64
BAD BOY BURRITO, 43
BAGATELLE, 43
BAHIA HONDA STATE PARK, 71
BANANA BAY RESORT & MARINA, 13
BANANA CAFÉ, 43
BANYAN RESORT, 17
BAREFOOT BILLY'S JET SKI TOURS, 90
BARRACUDA GRILL, 34
BEACHSIDE RESORT & CONFERENCE CENTER, 17
BIG CYPRESS NATIONAL PRESERVE, 64
Big Cypress Welcome Center, 64
BIG PINE BICYCLE CENTER, 99
BIG PINE KAYAK ADVENTURES, 72
BIG PINE TRUE VALUE BUILDERS SUPPLY, 99
BIPLANE TOURS, 92
BLUE EYED TRADER, 90
BLUE HEAVEN, 43
BLUE HOLE, 73
BLUE MARLIN MOTEL, 17
BLUE MOJITO POOL BAR & GRILL, 58
BOTTLECAP LOUNGE & LIQUOR STORE, 58
BOURBON STREET PUB, 59
Breakfast, 46
BUTTERFLY CAFÉ, 34

C

CABANA INN, 18
Cafe, 48
CAFÉ MARQUESA, 44
CAFÉ SOLÉ, 45
CAFÉ, A MOSTLY VEGETARIAN PLACE, 44
CALYPSO'S SEAFOOD GRILL, 34
CAPTAIN TONY'S SALOON, 59
Caribbean, 36
CASA MAR FRESH SEAFOOD MARKET, 99
CASA MARINA RESORT & BEACH CLUB, 18
CASA MORADA, 11
CHEECA LODGE & SPA, 11
CHEF MICHAEL'S, 34
CHELSEA HOUSE, 18
CLASSIC HARBOR LINE, 90
CLEARLY UNIQUE CHARTERS GLASS-BOTTOM KAYAKS, 91
CLINTON SQUARE MARKET, 100
COCKTAILS! KEY WEST, 100
COCO'S KITCHEN, 40
COCONUT PALM INN, 14
COMMODORE WATERFRONT, 45
COMPASS ROSE CHARTERS, 74
CONCH REPUBLIC SEAFOOD CO., 45
CONCH TOUR TRAIN, 74
CORK & STOGIE CIGAR AND WINE BAR, 59
COWBOY BILL'S HONKY TONK SALOON, 59
CRANE POINT HAMMOCK, 65
CROISSANTS DE FRANCE, 46
CROWNE PLAZA LA CONCHA, 19
Cuban, 46, 47, 56
CUBAN COFFEE QUEEN, 46
CURRY MANSION INN, 19
CURRY MANSION INN & MUSEUM, 75
CUSTOM HOUSE MUSEUM, 75
CYPRESS HOUSE, 19

D

D'VINE WINE GALLERY @ THE GARDENS HOTEL, 60
DAGNY JOHNSON HAMMOCK BOTANICAL STATE PARK, 65
DANCING DOLPHIN SPIRITS CHARTERS, 91
DANGER CHARTERS – WESTIN MARINA, 91
Deli, 56
DIVERS DIRECT OUTLET, 101
DJ'S CLAM SHACK, 46
DOLPHIN RESEARCH CENTER, 66
Donuts, 48
DOUBLETREE BY HILTON GRAND KEY RESORT, 20
DUFFY'S STEAK & LOBSTER HOUSE, 47
DUVAL INN, 20

E

EASY DAY CHARTERS, 92
EDEN HOUSE, 20
EQUATOR RESORT, 31
EVERGLADES ECO-TOURS, 66

EVERGLADES NATIONAL PARK, 63

F

FAIRFIELD INN & SUITES, 21
FAIRVILLA MEGASTORE, 101
FANTASY DAN AIR TOURS, 72
FANTASY FEST, 76
FARO BLANCO RESORT, 11
FAST BUCK'S AT HOME, 101
FAUSTO'S FOOD PALACE, 102
FISHING, 66
FIVE BROTHERS, 47
FLAGLER STATION & OVERSEAS RAILWAY HISTOREUM, 76
FLORIDA KEYS BREWING CO, 67
FLORIDA KEYS ECO-DISCOVERY CENTER, 76
FLORIDA KEYS OVERSEAS PADDLING TRAIL, 66
FLORIDA KEYS SEA SALT, 72
FLORIDA KEYS WILD BIRD CENTER, 67
FORT EAST MARTELLO, 77
Fort Jefferson, 89
FORT JEFFERSON TOURS, 78
FORT ZACHARY TAYLOR STATE PARK, 80
FRENCHIE'S CAFÉ, 48
FURY WATER ADVENTURES, 92

G

GARDEN OF EDEN, 60
GARDENS HOTEL, 21
GATES HOTEL, 21

GHOSTS & GRAVESTONES NIGHT TOUR, 81
GILBERT'S RESORT TIKI BAR, 35
GLAZED DONUTS, 48
GRAND GUESTHOUSE, 21
GRAND VIN WINE SHOP & BAR, 60
GREAT WHITE HERON NATIONAL WILDLIFE REFUGE, 72
GREEN PARROT BAR, 60
GREEN PINEAPPLE, 102
GREEN TURTLE INN, 35
Grocery, 47

H

HALF SHELL RAW BAR, 48
HARRIETTE'S RESTAURANT, 35
HAWK'S CAY RESORT, 11
HEMINGWAY HOME AND MUSEUM, 75
HISTORY OF DIVING MUSEUM, 67
HOG HEAVEN, 57
HOG'S BREATH SALOON, 61
Holiday Inn Docks, 66
HOT TIN ROOF, 48
HUNGRY TARPON, 36
HYDRO THUNDER WATERSPORTS HYATT, 93

I

ISLAMORADA FISH COMPANY, 36
ISLAND CITY HOUSE HOTEL, 22
ISLAND DOGS BAR, 49

ISLAND GRILL, 36
ISLAND HOUSE FOR MEN, 32
ISLAND SAFARI JET SKI TOURS, 94
ISLAND SMOKE SHOP, 97
ISLANDER RESORT, 12

J

JACOBS AQUATIC CENTER, 67
Jaw's Raw Bar, 14
JOHN PENNEKAMP CORAL REEF STATE PARK, 15, 68
JULES' UNDERSEA LODGE, 12

K

KAIYO GRILL & SUSHI, 36
KERMIT'S KEY WEST KEY LIME SHOPPE, 102
KEY LARGO CONCH HOUSE RESTAURANT & COFFEE BAR, 37
KEY WEST AQUARIUM, 81
KEY WEST ART & HISTORICAL SOCIETY, 82
KEY WEST BUTTERFLY & NATURE CONSERVATORY, 82
KEY WEST CEMETERY, 83
KEY WEST ECO TOURS, 93
KEY WEST FIREHOUSE MUSEUM, 83
KEY WEST GHOST & MYSTERIES TOURS, 84
KEY WEST GHOST TOUR, 83
Key West Harbour Yacht Club, 96
KEY WEST INTERNATIONAL HOSTEL, 28
KEY WEST ISLAND BOOKSTORE, 102
KEY WEST KEY LIME PIE CO., 103
KEY WEST LIGHTHOUSE MUSEUM, 84
KEY WEST SEAPLANES, 93
KEY WEST TROPICAL FOREST & BOTANICAL GARDEN, 85
KEY WEST WINERY, 103
KEYS FISHERIES MARKET & MARINA, 37
KEYS FRAMING & ART SUPPLIES, 103
KILWIN'S CHOCOLATES, 104
KMART, 97
KNOWLES HOUSE B&B, 23
KONA KAI RESORT & GALLERY, 12
KWEST LIQUORS, 104

L

LA PENSIONE, 23
LA TE DA, 23, 49, 61
LA TRATTORIA, 49
LATITUDES BEACH CAFÉ, 50
LAZY DAYS, 37
LAZY DOG KAYAK & PADDLEBOARD TOURS, 95
LIGHTHOUSE COURT, 24
LIME TREE BAY RESORT MOTEL, 15
LITTLE CONCH KEY PRIVATE ISLAND ESCAPE, 14
LONG KEY STATE PARK, 15
Looe Key Sanctuary Preservation Area, 71
LORELEI, 38
LOUIE'S BACKYARD, 50

M

M.V. KEY LARGO PRINCESS, 70
MALLORY SQUARE, 85
MANGIA, MANGIA, 50
MANGOES, 51
MANGROVE MAMA'S, 40
MARATHON KAYAK, 69
MARKER 88, 38
MARKER WATERFRONT RESORT, 24
MARQUESA HOTEL, 25
MARRIOTT BEACHSIDE HOTEL, 22
MARTIN'S, 51
MATTHEESSEN'S 4TH OF JULY ICE CREAM PARLOR, 51
MEL FISHER MARITIME HERITAGE MUSEUM, 86
MEL FISHER'S TREASURES, 104
MERMAID & THE ALIGATOR B&B, 25
MICHAEL'S RESTAURANT, 52
MICHELLE NICOLE LOWE ART GALLERY, 69
Mile Marker Address System, 6
MOORINGS VILLAGE, 13
MORADA BAY BEACH CAFÉ, 13
MR Z'S, 52

N

NAILTINI NAIL BAY & DAY SPA, 104
National Key Deer Refuge, 6
NATIONAL KEY DEER REFUGE, 73
NEW ORLEANS HOUSE, 32
NINE ONE FIVE BISTRO & WINE BAR, 53
NO NAME PUB, 41

O

Oasis Visitor Center, 64
Ocean Key Resort & Spa, 48
OCEAN KEY RESORT AND SPA, 25
OLD TOWN FITNESS, 106
OLD TOWN MANOR & ROSE LANE VILLAS, 26
OLD TOWN TROLLEY TOURS, 86
ONLYWOOD PIZZERIA TRATTORIA, 53

P

PANINI PANINI, 53
PARADISE PILATES, 106
PARMER'S RESORT, 16
PEPE'S, 53
PEPPERS OF KEY WEST, 105
PIER HOUSE, 26
PIERRE'S, 39
PILATES STUDIO OF KEY WEST, 106
PINES AND PALMS, 15
POSTCARD INN BEACH RESORT & MARINA, 14

R

RAGGED EDGE RESORT, 16
RAIN BARREL VILLAGE, 97
REACH RESORT, 26
RED BARN THEATRE, 86

RICK'S & DURTY HARRY'S, 61
RIPLEY'S BELIEVE IT OR NOT, 87
ROBBIE'S OF ISLAMORADA, 70
RUM BAR AT THE SPEAKEASY INN, 62

S

SailorsChoice, 66
SAINT HOTEL KEY WEST, 27
SANDAL FACTORY, 98
SANDY'S CAFÉ, 54
SANTA MARIA SUITES, 27
SANTIAGO'S BODEGA, 54
SARABETH'S, 55
Schooner Wharf Bar, 90
SCHOONER WHARF BAR, 62
Seafood, 34, 36, 48
SEAPLANE TOURS, 80
SEASCAPE, 27
SEASHELL MOTEL, 28
SEBAGO WATERSPORTS, 95
SEVEN FISH, 55
SHELL WORLD, 98
SHIPWRECK HISTOREUM, 84
SHIPWRECK TREASURES MUSEUM, 87
Shula Burger, 14
SILVER PALMS INN, 28
SIMONTON COURT, 28
SMOKIN' TUNA SALOON, 62
SNAPPER'S, 39
SOUTHERNMOST HOTEL, 28
SOUTHERNMOST HOUSE, 29
SOUTHERNMOST HOUSE & MUSEUM, 88
SOUTHERNMOST POINT GUEST HOUSE, 29
SPEAKEASY INN, 29

Speed Traps, 6
SUNSET WATERSPORTS, 95

T

TAVERN N TOWN, 55
THAI CUISINE, 56
THEATER OF THE SEA, 70
Tiki Bar, 14
TIKI BAR AT THE HOLIDAY ISLE RESORT, 57
TRANQUILITY BAY BEACH HOUSE RESORT, 13
TRANSPORTARTION AND TIPS FOR GETTING AROUND, 6
TRAVELER'S PALM, 30
TROPIC CINEMA, 88
TRUMAN HOTEL, 30
TRUMAN'S LITTLE WHITE HOUSE, 81
TURTLE HOSPITAL, 70
TURTLE KRAALS, 56

V

Vegan, 34
Vegetarian, 34
VENUS CHARTERS, 96
VILLAS KEY WEST, 30

W

WESTWINDS INN, 30
WHEELS-2-GO, 71
WHITE STREET SANDWICH SHOP, 56
WILD ABOUT DOLPHINS, 96
WOODY'S SALOON AND RESTAURANT, 58

WRECKER'S MUSEUM - THE OLDEST HOUSE IN KEY WEST, 88, 89

Z

ZIGGIE AND MAD DOG'S, 40

Y

YANKEE FREEDOM II **DAY TRIPS**, 79

A few of the other books by the Author

THE ADVENTURES OF SHERLOCK HOLMES IV

In this series, the original Sherlock Holmes's great-great-great grandson solves crimes and mysteries in the present day, working out of the boutique hotel he owns on South Beach.

THE BOSCOMBE VALLEY MYSTERY

Sherlock Holmes and Watson are called to a remote area of Florida overlooking Lake Okeechobee to investigate a murder where all the evidence points to the victim's son as the killer. Holmes, however, is not so sure.

THE DEVIL'S FOOT

Holmes's doctor orders him to take a short holiday in Key West, and while there, Holmes is called on to look into a case in which three people involved in a Santería ritual died with no explanation.

THE CLEVER ONE

A former nun who, while still very devout, has renounced her vows so that she could "find a life, and possibly love, in the real world." She comes to Holmes in hopes that he can find out what happened to the man who promised to marry her, but mysteriously disappeared moments before their wedding.

THE COPPER BEECHES

A nanny reaches out to Sherlock Holmes seeking his advice on whether she should take a new position when her prospective employer has demanded that she cut her hair as part of the job.

THE RED-HAIRED MAN

A man with a shock of red hair calls on Sherlock Holmes to solve the mystery of the Red-haired League.

THE SIX NAPOLEONS

Inspector Lestrade calls on Holmes to help him figure out why a madman would go around Miami breaking into homes and businesses to destroy cheap busts of the French Emperor. It all seems very insignificant to Holmes—until, of course, a murder occurs.

THE MAN WITH THE TWISTED LIP

In what seems to be the case of a missing person, Sherlock Holmes navigates his way through a maze of perplexing clues that leads him through a sinister world to a surprising conclusion.

THE BORNHOLM DIAMOND

A mysterious Swedish nobleman requests a meeting to discuss a matter of such serious importance that it may threaten the line of succession in one of the oldest royal houses in Europe.

www.ingramcontent.com/pod-product-compliance
Lightning Source LLC
Chambersburg PA
CBHW071714040426
42446CB00011B/2059